Funny LaDies

The Women Who Make Us Laugh

by Stephen M. Silverman

Harry N. Abrams, Inc., Publishers

**TO GLADYS ROBIN PELTZ JOSEPHSON JAFFE POLL,
WHO NEVER BOTHERS TO BE NICE.
SHE'S TOO BUSY BEING FUNNY.**

Editor: Ruth A. Peltason
Designer: Molly Shields

Page 1: Polly Moran; *page 3:* Carol Burnett; *page 4:* from *I Love Lucy*; *page 5:* Lucille Ball; *page 7:* Jean Arthur; *page 8:* Pearl Bailey; *page 9:* Cher and Martha Raye

Library of Congress Cataloging-in-Publication Data
Silverman, Stephen M.
      Funny ladies : the women who make us laugh / by Stephen M. Silverman.
          p.   cm.
      Includes bibliographical references and index.
      ISBN 0–8109–3337–3
      1. Women comedians—United States—Biography.   I. Title.
PN2285.S533   1999
792.7'028'0820973
[B]—DC21   99–11058

Printed and bound in Japan

 Harry N. Abrams, Inc.
100 Fifth Avenue
New York, N.Y. 10011
www.abramsbooks.com

contents

Histc
actor ever
cross-eyec
(Some cla
from the L
her right p
feet, went
    Mabe
born eithe
an itinerar
girl to rais
others arg
What has
Island. "He
she learne
    At ac
feet and s
poster for
James Mor
Manhattan
Griffith anc
"looked lik
    Shifti
opened his
comedies.
an oil slic
one anoth
and turne
tossing a
her, bump
shoving he
love. Such
1915, whe
Sennett's a
Mae Bush,
go work fc
    Not tl
same blusl
had met se
conversatic
Her profes
two highly
director Wi

> "Being a funny person does an awful lot of things to you. You feel that you mustn't get serious with people. They don't expect it from you, and they don't want to see it. You're not entitled to be serious, you're a clown, and they only want you to make them laugh."
>
> —Fanny Brice

A gifted mimic, a gut-wrenching torch singer, and an ill-fated lover whose romantic entanglements were the stuff of moviemakers' residuals, Fanny Brice (1891–1951), above all, had *presence*—and prescience. "So many things she said stopped you cold," declared the century's great chronicler, Ben Hecht, referring to Brice's psychic gift. "She was about people the way those carnival fellows are about your weight." Fanny *was* intuitive: "I never worked out any business ahead of time," she declared of her performance technique. "It would only happen when I hit the audience, because they speak so much louder than my mind."

So perhaps it was her second sight that in 1905 led the fourteen-year-old Fannie Borach—the refinements in the name came later—to her first amateur contest. The setting (as accurately identified in the most famous Brice film bio, 1968's widescreen *Funny Girl**) was the unceremonious Keeney's Theater in Brooklyn, across the East River from Brice's native Lower East Side. The gawky teen warbled "When You Know You're Not Forgotten by the Girl You Can't Forget" and took home the top prize: ten dollars.

The Brice household was the springboard for Fanny's extroversion. Papa, a ne'er-do-well Alsatian immigrant named Charles Borach (a.k.a. "Pinochle Charlie"), owned several saloons—at least they were in his name. Their actual management was handled by his wife, the Hungarian-born Rose Stern. "He liked his liquor," Fanny recalled of the

Opposite: *Brice started on radio in 1932, introducing a bratty four-year-old character called "Baby Snooks" (clowning here with George Burns and Gracie Allen at Brice's 1939 birthday party). Created by Fanny at a party in 1921, Snooks's distinctive voice—whining "Why-y-y, Daddy?"—was the product of the lisp Brice developed when her dentures broke.*

Left: *Fanny Brice in 1910, the year she debuted in* The Ziegfeld Follies.

14yrs

* Besides the gussied-up *Funny Girl*, the Brice-Arnstein saga also inspired the 1939 Alice Faye–Tyrone Power musical *Rose of Washington Square*, which was so close to the true story that Brice successfully sued Twentieth Century-Fox for invasion of privacy.

officially exonerated). The other took place on January 1, 1924, when Mabel's chauffeur shot the Hollywood millionaire Courtland S. Dines at his mansion while Mabel was on the premises.

On September 17, 1926, a fragile Mabel Normand married the debonair screen star Lew Cody at four in the morning, after a party. She had tuberculosis and pneumonia; he had a heart ailment. Mabel died in 1930, Cody in 1934.

SILENT STARS
PIONEER SPIRITS

Vulgarity being a Mack Sennett trademark, the filmmaker was fortunate that early motion picture cameras were not attuned to capturing subtlety of gesture or character. Nor were audiences of the day necessarily attuned to appreciating them. Sennett mastered broad farce by casting physical "types": Fatty Arbuckle (corpulent, babylike), Slim Summerville (cadaverous), Ben Turpin (cross-eyed), Chester Conklin (walrus-mustached), and Ford Serling (pop-eyed, scrunch-faced).

Sennett gave equal time to women, especially his popular **Bathing Beauties,** who were exploited more for their physical attributes than for any gift for physical comedy. Sennett's female headliners included:

* The portly and snaggle-toothed **Polly Moran,** who, starting in 1917, played the ongoing burlesque Western character Sheriff Nell

* The adaptable **Minta Durfee** (Arbuckle's real-life wife and early leading lady), who could muster sympathy or hilarity, depending upon the situation

* And **Louise Fazenda,** a gawky Hoosier who joined Sennett in 1915 and became the number-one favorite slapstick actress of the silent era. Invariably cast as the farmer's tomboy daughter—Sennett had her trademark pigtails insured for $10,000—she also grimaced her way through some three hundred films, in roles ranging from an American Indian to a blacksmith, before she retired in the late thirties.

Mack Sennett did not hold the patent on silent comedy. At Universal Studios, under the then production chief Irving G. Thalberg, frizzy-haired Alice Howell enjoyed the reputation of each and every one of her films being a "Howell." Puns aside, Stan Laurel considered Howell the screen's funniest star, male or female.

*"I'm a bagel or
rolls," Barbra S
the best of the
often-effective I
stage in 1964
1968, followea
torpid Funny L
classy perfectio
as Snooks, witl
Ziegfeld Follie:
was a rich, del*

* He had played the bad guy in *Mickey.*

BABY
ask
WOI
DADD'
BABY
"S|

By 1910 Dressler made a name for herself in New York and London for her stage role of houseworker Tillie Blobbs in the comic play *Tillie's Nightmare,* which Mack Sennett, making his first feature-length picture, filmed in Hollywood four years later as *Tillie's Punctured Romance.** Tightwad Sennett squawked when he had to ante up an unprecedented (for him) $35,000 to enlist Dressler's services, but the investment paid off: the film was a hit and established Dressler as a Hollywood star. Woodrow Wilson, an avid movie fan, welcomed her to the White House, while in France, American GIs honored Dressler by naming both a street and a cow after her.**

With *Tillie's* success, Dressler followed with two sequels, neither for Sennett nor for much of an audience. Similarly, Dressler's theatrical opportunities dried up thanks to her active pro–Actors Equity stance in a 1919 stage strike. By 1925, the venerable star grandly announced her retirement. In truth, she took to selling real estate and, at her lowest point, to hawking peanuts in Coney Island.

What brought her back was having a fan at M-G-M, the screenwriter Frances Marion. (Dressler had done her a great favor years before, when Marion was a cub reporter for Hearst and needed a name interview.) Marion wrote the feuding-neighbor comedy *The Callahans and the Murphys* for Dressler and Polly Moran in 1927, leading M-G-M to sign Marie—and, in 1930, co-star her opposite Greta Garbo as the drinking crony in the legend's first talkie, *Anna Christie.* When the studio paired the old trouper with Wallace Beery as the scrappy dockside slum dwellers *Min and Bill* (1930, written by Marion), Dressler earned the Best Actress Oscar and the cover of *Time.*

Her most memorable role came in 1933, the same year she played the lead in *Tugboat Annie* and one year before her death. In the delectable *Dinner at Eight,* Dressler was the queen of London's West End, the retired

* It starred Charlie Chaplin (before he perfected the look of his mustache), as a city slicker charmed by Dressler's bumpkin Tillie, and Mabel Normand as Charlie's incredulous girlfriend.
** When the cow was killed during World War I, Dressler woke up to national headlines proclaiming "'MARIE DRESSLER' KILLED IN LINE OF DUTY." Said the two-legged Marie: "I had a hard time convincing people that the report of my death had been greatly exaggerated."

Dressler (camping it up in Hollywood Revue of 1929) was married once, possibly twice. First came George Hoppert, in 1900, though shortly after the wedding he became an invalid and died. Fourteen years later, she was said to have married her manager, James H. Dalton, but no marriage license confirming the union ever existed. Dalton died in 1921 and Dressler devotedly visited his grave, which may have given rise to the supposition they were wed.

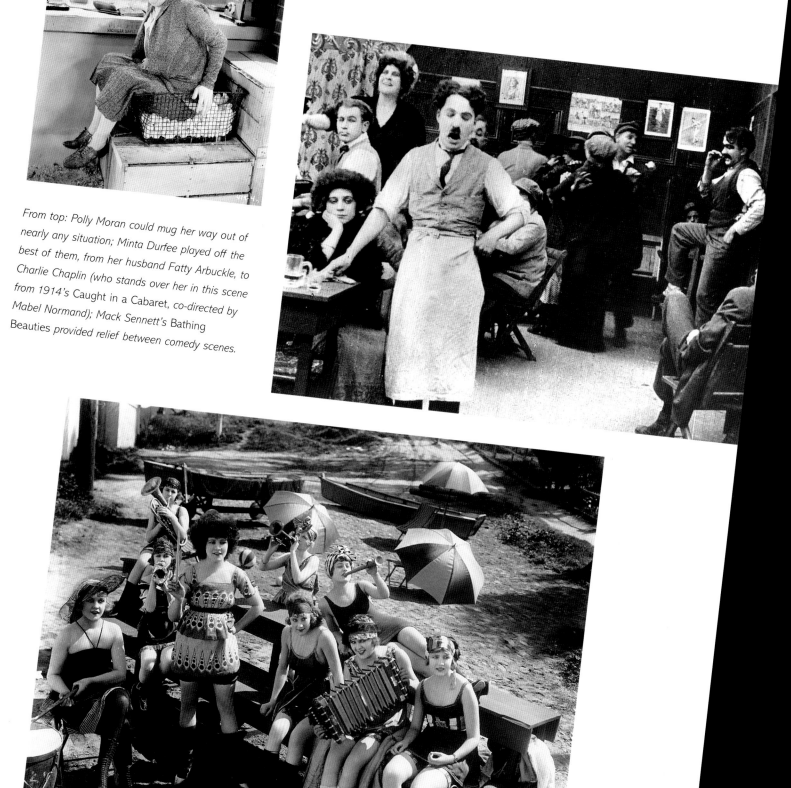

From top: Polly Moran could mug her way out of nearly any situation; Minta Durfee played off the best of them, from her husband Fatty Arbuckle, to Charlie Chaplin (who stands over her in this scene from 1914's Caught in a Cabaret, co-directed by Mabel Normand); Mack Sennett's Bathing Beauties provided relief between comedy scenes.

Louise Fazenda, after her days as a box-office draw, became a social activist. (In 1925 she married the producer Hal B. Wallis, who later became head of production for Warner Bros.) During the time of the Nazi persecutions in Europe she helped bring Jewish refugees to the safe haven of Baja, California. "She proved a true comedian," Rabbi Morton Bauman said at her funeral in 1962, "not one who knew only the flippancies of life but one who knew life in all dimensions."

MARIE DRESSLER
DOWAGER EMPRESS

Never one to be coy, Marie Dressler didn't just make a name for herself in show business, she stole one. Born Leila Marie Koreber in Coburg, Ontario, Canada, in 1869, Dressler had parents who didn't mind if their ungainly daughter entertained on the stage, just so long as she didn't use the family name. Taking the identity of a long-deceased aunt, Leila became Marie Dressler.

Dressler's face was her fortune, and what a face it was! She admitted to bearing a strong resemblance to Prussia's William I—others might suggest she was the role model for J. Edgar Hoover in drag—and, having acted with Dressler in one drama, Maurice Barrymore unhesitatingly advised that comedy was her forte. She became a Broadway headliner after "eleven years of tank towns and hard work and little pay—sometimes no pay at all," she recalled in her 1924 au telling called *The Life Story of an Ugly Duckling.*

that she was a great actress, then reversed their roles, giving Gracie the funny lines and himself the straight ones. He would play the sexual wolf, and Gracie would escape his advances by just being too darned silly to understand them. Exasperation (his) led to hilarity. Professionally they were launched.

At the time, Gracie was set to marry the Irish songwriter-dancer Benny Ryan, except that when Gracie was hospitalized for an emergency appendectomy, she asked George to notify Ryan. He didn't. George, meanwhile, surrounded her hospital bed with flowers—and threatened that, even though religious differences existed between them,* if she didn't marry him he would dissolve the act. This led to an argument and Gracie's reportedly calling George the next morning to say he could go buy the ring.

"You're the only boy who ever made me cry," she told him. "And I decided that if you could make me cry, I must really love you."

They were married on January 7, 1926. As she told a friend (on radio):

GRACIE: I don't want a husband with money and good looks and personality. I'd rather have George. And I'm not the only one who feels that way. Plenty of women have told me how relieved they are that he's with me.

"Time wounds all heels," was a typical Jane Ace malapropism. "We're all cremated equal" was another—and better—one. Here Jane and husband Goodman Ace go to the track, assisted by radio announcer Clem McCarthy, who was famous for his growly greeting, "Good afternoon, r-r-racing fans."

JANE ACE
MISS MALAPROP

A somewhat earthier version of *Burns and Allen*—in that the show's married leads didn't mind airing their marital differences—was Goodman and Jane Ace's *Easy Aces,* which started on radio in 1933, a year after George and Gracie's wireless debut. The Aces (born Goodman Aiskowitz and Jane Epstein) began with a fifteen-minute, thrice-a-week show out of New York, though by 1943 their format shifted over to the standard half-hour sitcom of the day. Goodie, as he was known, would gladly suffer Jane's malapropisms ("I'd like to go on the stage. You know, the thrill of getting behind the footnotes, the smell of the goose grease, seeing my name up in tights"), and the show even made it to early television. But Goodman's real ace in the hole was his writing. Once Jane retired in 1950 (she died in 1974, aged seventy-four; he died at age eighty-three in 1982), Goodie became one of radio and television's top comedy writers, at one point earning $10,000 a week putting funny words into the mouths of Tallulah Bankhead, Perry Como, and Sid Caesar.

* The Jewish Burns was born Nathan Birnbaum. Gracie was an Irish Catholic.

discovered this the hard way while playing opposite her in the 1936 *The Show Is On*. The script called for him to stride up to a ticket window on stage, ask for a seat, then break into some comic banter with Lillie, who played the cashier. "Well," he remembered, "one night when I stepped up, she slammed the window in my face and shouted, 'So sorry. Box office closed.'"

Actually, the very English Beatrice Gladys Lillie (1894–1989) was born in Toronto, Canada, the younger of two daughters. Her father, John Lillie, an official with the Canadian government, had served with the British army in India before he married Lucie Shaw, who was of Spanish and English extraction. "Four Lillies were enough for any bouquet," Bea said of her family tree. Her parents believed Beatrice would become an opera singer, but she lacked the discipline. Her problem, besides a lifelong contempt of anything grand, was that she had discovered the joy of getting a laugh. At age eight she was expelled from her church choir for causing the boys to giggle by making funny faces and flapping her fan during the sermon.

The young eccentric once tried to win a piano by entering a singing contest in a Toronto burlesque house. (The effort did not please her mother.) At fifteen, Bea sailed for England, where Mrs. Lillie had taken her elder daughter, Muriel, to study music. But it was Beatrice who found her way to the stage. Her first appearance, which ran a week, was as a male impersonator in top hat and tails. "I was," she later boasted, "the best-dressed transvestite in the world."

Of the many adoring stage-door Johnnies who came a-calling, she fell the hardest for the handsome Sir Robert Peel, whose ancestor (also named Sir Robert Peel) served as one of Queen Victoria's prime ministers and organized London's Metropolitan police force.* In 1920, Robert and Beatrice married at the Peel estate, Drayton Manor, in a ceremony notable for the absence of the bridegroom's parents, who disapproved of theatrical folk.

The newlyweds' only child, also named Robert and called Little Bobbie, was born a year later, by which time Beatrice was ready to return to the stage. It wasn't simply that she was bored at home, though she was, but that Robert senior was a gambler who could scarcely hold a job. In time, husband and wife grew apart, and in 1934, Sir Robert, age thirty-six, died of peritonitis in the bed of his mistress. Six years later, Little Bobbie, who had enlisted in the Royal Navy, was killed during a Japanese air raid on the port of Colombo, Ceylon. Ever the trouper, Lillie, who was performing in the show *Big Top* that day, posted a notice to her fellow actors backstage: "I know how you all feel. Don't let's talk about it. Bless you. Now let's get on with our work."

Lillie spent much of the war entertaining troops around the Mediterranean, in Africa, the Middle East, and, later, Germany. "Anyone who ever saw her sketch about a slightly tipsy, tongue-tied Mrs. Blagdon Blogg turning Harrods department store in London into a state of havoc would consider her an adorably nutty fool," said the *New York Times*. In the skit, Mrs. Blogg stumbled with her order of "two

* Its members—"bobbies"—were named for him.

"Wit has truth in it; wisecracking is simply calisthenics with words."
—Dorothy Parker

Parker married twice-and-a-half; first, in 1917, to Edwin Pond Parker, a stockbroker (they divorced in 1928), then, in 1934, to the handsome Alan Campbell, with whom she collaborated on screenplays, including the original 1937 *A Star Is Born*. The Campbells ultimately divorced, then remarried in 1950, only to separate again for eleven years before reuniting in 1962. While some biographers have portrayed Parker as a sad and lonely figure—"a masochist whose passion for unhappiness knows no bounds," a friend told one Boswell—and literary critics may have dismissed her serious essays as self-pitying, Parker will forever remain part of the American lexicon if for no other reason than her wry, nine-word observation about the dating habits of the species, "Men seldom make passes at girls who wear glasses."

BEATRICE LILLIE
THE CONSTANT IMP

The pillbox hat was a Beatrice Lillie trademark. So was a rapier wit.

A spring day in New York. An East End Avenue apartment wi
wide open. And, suddenly, a pigeon flies in and alights on
living-room chair. The feathered intruder ruffles most of th
the lady of the house. Fixing the bird with her gaze, Beatrice Lill
messages?"

Over a fifty-year career, the sprightly Miss Lillie earned the
Funniest Woman in the World" and "The Toast of Two Continer
boasted a true title, that of Lady Peel. Sporting a trademark er
hat and boyish bob, Lillie knew precisely how to accentuate he
impromptu barbs wi
extended cigarette l
whoosh of a looooo
pearls hula-hooping
"I find the exercise
said of the pearl ro
there's always a ce
getting started, of
front teeth."

An intimate of
Winston Churchill, C
George Bernard Sh
reeked of style. To
she sent a live rhin
Harrods, along with
what else is new?'

Whether on s
London in 1914 ar
the sophisticated l
Revue of 1924), or
silents, a cameo ir
Eighty Days, then
type as a white sl
Modern Millie), or
talk-show host Me
her rendition of C
Party"), the icono
frequently said, n
same performanc

Above: *"She didn't drink a drop,"* Sir John Mills remembered of Beatrice Lillie (here in a publicity shot, circa mid-1930s), *"except later in life she liked her lager. She took to drinking it directly out of this large jug she always kept at her side."* As for her performance: *"Once she sang a song, she burlesqued it so, no one else would dare ever touch it again."*

Right: *The Gospel According to St. Sophie:* "From birth to age eighteen, a girl needs good parents. From eighteen to thirty-five, she needs good looks. From thirty-five to fifty-five, she needs good personality. From fifty-five on, she needs good cash."

dozen double-damask dinner napkins," a request that soon started coming out of her mouth as "two dazzle dimask dibble dammer nipples."

Another standard in her repertoire, the Edwardian drawing-room ballad "There Are Fairies in the Bottom of My Garden," was first heard by her friend Ethel Barrymore, who found it lovely and serious. Beatrice showed her. Lillie delivered the ditty draped in a long formal gown . . . before she raised her skirt and roller-skated off stage.

In person, Lillie, who called her 1972 autobiography *Every Other Inch a Lady,* took special delight in deflating the pompous. To imperious headwaiters in fancy restaurants she would peer over the top of her menu and demurely request "Rice Krispies." Then there was the time she and several chorus girls were in a Chicago beauty parlor before the opening of a show. Mrs. Armour, wife of the owner of the canned meat company, entered and informed the salon's proprietor that she was "mortified and infuriated to learn this establishment has been taken over by showgirls." A perfect setup for Beatrice Lillie. As the star left her booth, she loudly proclaimed for the edification of all: "You may tell the butcher's wife that Lady Peel has finished."

SOPHIE TUCKER
SCHMALTZ APPEAL

S ophie Tucker was a strange amalgam: part Jewish mother, part dirty old lady. She inspired as many other entertainers as she turned off those outraged by her ribaldry or, worse, her gushing sentimentality. But the former Sophia Kalish (Louis Tuck, whom she wed at the age of sixteen, was only around long enough to give her the stage name) was good-

natured and the last of a breed, the "Red Hot Mama" who didn't stop belting suggestive numbers such as "I May Be Getting Older Every Day, but Getting Younger Every Night" until the very last hand in the audience ached from applauding.

Sophie's shtick was presenting herself, despite her two-hundred-pound girth, as a self-believing sex bomb, a reputation she encouraged with comic patter and bawdy songs, generally penned by her favorite songwriter, Fred Fish. A typical Fish refrain, in this instance about a pregnant secretary demanding payment from her boss for putting out: "When am I getting my mink, Mr. Fink?"

In 1914, at age thirty, Sophie made the professional leap from her Polish-immigrant parents' restaurant in Hartford, Connecticut, to vaudeville's mecca, Broadway's Palace Theater, and she kept on performing until her death in 1966. The secret of her career longevity—until such time as she became a self-parody—was the way she elicited laughter with her quips one minute and tears with her ballads the next.*

From a performance standpoint, Sophie operated on the same two-way street that Bette Midler maneuvered with hipper finesse in the latter's concerts starting in the 1970s. Midler also claimed to tell "Soph" stories, truly filthy jokes that truthfully were not from the Sophie Tucker cannon but which certainly *could* have been—and which nevertheless made the late Tucker a revitalized legend in her own right. The best of Midler's "Soph" jokes involved Sophie's boyfriend Ernie telling her in bed one night, "Soph, you got no tits and a tight box." To which Sophie said, "Ernie, get off my back."

MAE WEST
SEX SYMBOL

With her hourglass figure that took on a lot more sand as the years wore on, her garish wardrobe of spangles and furs, and her peculiar gift for sexual innuendo, Mae West was a living landmark, a Fourth of July firecracker that sparkled every day of the year. Her heyday spanned the twenties and spilled over into the early thirties, when as the embodiment of the character she created, Diamond Lil (an amalgamation of two profligate turn-of-the-century personalities, the actress Lillian Russell and "Diamond Jim" Brady, the tycoon who showered Russell with jewels), the sin-promising West shook Puritan sensibilities to their roots—and she grabbed a whole lot of publicity doing it.

"It isn't what I do, but how I do it," she said in her purring tough-girl voice. (Chaplin, it was said, admired the ease and persuasiveness of her delivery.) "It isn't what I say, but how I say it, and how I look when I do it and say it." Given her independent spirit, she was often credited for being an early feminist. Not that

---

* So sentimental was Tucker that Eddie Cantor was forced to observe, "Sophie would cry at a card trick."

For her first film, the 1932 Night After Night: "I walked into George Raft's fashionable clipjoint, and the checkroom girl [Alison Skipworth] took one look at all the diamonds I was wearing and exclaimed, 'Goodness, what beautiful diamonds!' 'Goodness had nothing to do with it, dearie,' I replied." West dropped the "dearie" from the expression and used that as the title of her 1959 autobiography. Here is the star in 1935 with Harry Dean, of the Los Angeles District Attorney's Office. He's done up in order to capture an extortion suspect who was bothering West at the time.

WESTISMS

* "Keep a diary, and someday it'll keep you."
* "I was born Snow White, but I drifted."
* "It's better to be looked over than overlooked."
* "Too much of a good thing can be wonderful."
* "I'm not good and tired, just tired."
* "Sex is an emotion in motion."
* "Between two evils I always pick the one I never tried before."
* "I've been on more laps than a napkin."
* "When a woman goes bad, men go right after her."
* "Men like women with a past, because they hope history will repeat itself."
* "I've been things and seen places."
* "When I'm good I'm very good, when I'm bad I'm better."
* But she never did say, "Come up and see me sometime." She said, "Come up sometime. See me."

West cared to dabble in sexual politics. Her game was *simply* sex, and to hell with the politics. Mae West didn't need to make her presence felt in a man's world, because, in her plays and movies, the world didn't belong to them. It belonged to her. For Mae West, who was married only once and then briefly, the opposite sex existed merely as a means to satisfy her own carnal and materialistic desires.*

"Love," the diva professed, "is a woman's stock-in-trade, and she should always be overstocked."

Because her personality was so exaggerated it was often theorized that West was really a man in drag—a ridiculous assumption, although as she became a hopeless self-parody in her old age, less impossible to discount. Despite her tiny physical frame, barely five-foot in her fish-net-stockinged feet, nothing about the woman was life-sized. The perfect West setting? A brawling honky-tonk. The seemingly perfect West foil? W. C. Fields,

playing the hard-hearted cynic to her oversexed siren. (They co-starred in only one film, the less-than-hoped-for *My Little Chickadee,* and their personalities clashed so that they shared few scenes together.) The perfect leading man? The tall, dark, and handsome Cary Grant, whom West discovered *(I'm No Angel,* 1933). Seeing the actor walking down one of the streets on the Paramount lot, she said, "If he can talk, I'll take him." Imagine, she gave the world Cary Grant. She also was the first to introduce the shimmy to the stage and broke new ground with her relationships with blacks in her movies (her maids were less servants than they were friends and confidantes). All that, and she was the single reason Hollywood instituted the Legion of Decency.

Born in Brooklyn on August 17, 1892—her birth sign was that of the virgin, and she never smoked or drank—Mary Jane West made her first stage appearance before the turn of the century. She was the first of three children of John Patrick West, an occasional prizefighter and livery-stable owner, and Matilda Delker Doelger, a former corset and fashion model. Little blond Mae took dancing lessons and then participated in the first of many amateur-night performances at Brooklyn's Royal Theater on Fulton Street. Outfitted in a pink and green satin dress with gold

* Materially, West excelled. In 1934, as Paramount Pictures' biggest star, her $480,000 annual paycheck was said to be the second-highest salary in the country, after William Randolph Hearst's ($500,000). She shrewdly invested in Los Angeles real estate.

spangles, she sang and danced "Movin' Day" with what she later termed "innocent brazenness." She took first prize.

She was thirteen when she entered vaudeville, and at eighteen she secretly married a song-and-dance man on the bill, Frank Wallace. "Miss West then developed a single act, helped Mr. Wallace find a job with a show that was going on the road for forty weeks, and thus informally dissolved both her professional and conjugal unions," recorded the *New York Times.* She never married again.

Gaining experience rewriting her material and stopping shows—West had a knack for being constantly prepared with another song verse—she turned to playwriting with a 1926 debut piece called *Sex,* which she directed and starred in, as the prostitute Margy LaMont. The show featured a bordello setting and was produced by West, her beloved mother, Matilda, and James Timony, a lawyer who became West's manager and longtime associate. "I only knew two rules of playwriting," West said. "Write about what you know, and make it entertaining."

When *Sex* opened in New York in April 1926, the city's papers refused to carry ads for it. Not that the box office suffered. Even more fortuitous was the arrest of West on obscenity charges and the high-profile trial that followed. The jury found West guilty of a performance that "tended to corrupt the morals of youth and others" and she was fined five hundred dollars and sentenced to ten days in prison.

The following year she wrote and directed (but didn't star in) a play about homosexuality called *The Drag.* Despite its being a hit in Paterson, New Jersey,

During World War II, West's name was applied to various pieces of military equipment and was listed as such in Webster's New International Dictionary, *Second Edition.* The Royal Air Force named its inflatable life jackets "Mae Wests" and United States Army soldiers referred to twin-turreted combat tanks as "Mae Wests." Said the star, "I've been in Who's Who and I know what's what, but that's the first time I ever made the dictionary." She died in 1980.

she was warned against bringing it into New York. (West did not become rich by ignoring sage advice.)

In 1928 came *Diamond Lil,* about a bawdy singer in a Bowery saloon of the 1890s: "a bad girl with a good heart, who murdered her girlfriend, wrecked a Salvation Army hall, and sang 'Frankie and Johnny,'" reported the *New York Times.* The show ran for 323 performances in New York and then went on national tour. "I hadn't started out to collect diamonds," said Li, "but somehow they piled up on me." Seldom was there a more willing victim.

MARION DAVIES
HISTORY'S CHILD

"She was very gay and very warm," Hearst journalist Adela Rogers St. John remembered of Marion Davies (photographed here in 1931). "And, of course, she wore diamonds. She had a lot of diamonds."

For a 1996 documentary called *Welles and Hearst,* Orson Welles, who died in 1985, was shown saying he "did Marion Davies an enormous disservice." Talk about gross understatement. In Welles's brilliant but barely veiled 1941 portrait of publisher William Randolph Hearst, *Citizen Kane,* the prodigal filmmaker depicted the blond mistress of the ruthless, lonely publisher Charles Foster Kane as a shrill, talentless alcoholic. Granted, the character in the movie, named Susan Alexander, was an opera singer and not a movie star, but the public knew ruthless, friendless Kane was passing for Hearst and that former Ziegfeld Follies chorine Marion Davies (1897–1961) was his paramour. Friends of Davies also knew that Marion, like the Susan Alexander character, was never far from a bottle, and there was something extra cruel about making her *Kane* character a singer given the fact Marion stuttered, a setback that had kept her out of talkies.

While it could not be said that the *Kane* connection damaged Davies's career, which she herself ended three years prior to the release of the picture, her reputation consequently suffered in the years since.

Revisionists, on the other hand, have long risen to Davies's defense, believing she was a talented artist who, given her natural agility and photogenic features, could have scaled the heights even without the financial aid of "the Chief." Their strongest argument is M-G-M's 1928 *Show People,* a silent movie that lampooned the career—and ego—of Gloria Swanson, not as completely as *Kane* took on Hearst, but far more good-naturedly. Davies excelled in scenes that allowed her to mimic the grand manner of the screen queen, though Hearst much preferred to see his Marion play innocent virgins. That, coupled with movie exhibitors' antagonism over Hearst's high-handed promotion of Marion's pictures, deprived the movies of what could possibly have been an enduring funny lady.

MARGARET DUMONT
MARXIST

Her performances were wooden, she sang like a cross between a Jeanette Macdonald impersonator and a rooster, and her demeanor smacked of uptight society biddy. Yet Margaret Dumont was a goddess created by the Marx Brothers comedies. Whether enduring Groucho's endless barrage of digs—it

Groucho Marx with Margaret Dumont in possibly their best movie together, the 1935 A Night at the Opera. *(Purists prefer their 1933* Duck Soup.) *Receiving the check at the dinner table, Groucho exclaims, "Nine-forty! This is an outrage." He then hands the bill to Dumont. "If I were you, I wouldn't pay it."*

THELMA TODD AND PATSY KELLY
FIRECRACKER AND WISECRACKER

As the only truly sexy foil who could contend with Groucho Marx, **Thelma TOdd** enjoys the dubious distinction of having had the mustached master sing his cockeyed lyrics to "Everyone Says I Love You" to her in a rowboat in 1932's *Horse Feathers*—while *she* was rowing the boat. Movie fans will no doubt better recall the good-natured beauty for putting up with the Marxes's beastliness* than they will for her series of comedy shorts with ZaSu Pitts and, later, with Patsy Kelly, for which she was more justly celebrated in her time but which, in the decades since, have faded from sight.

Pert and vivacious, Todd represents one of the great sorrowful stories of Hollywood. She was born in Lawrence, Massachusetts, in 1905 and came to movies in the twenties. By the mid-thirties there was every reason to believe the former Miss Massachusetts, who'd risen through the studio ranks via silent comedies with Charlie Chase and Harry Langdon, would be giving Carole Lombard a good run for the better comedy parts. Instead, Todd died in 1935 of carbon monoxide poisoning behind the wheel of her car while it was parked inside her own garage. The coroner said suicide. Yet her mother, pointing to injuries on Todd's face and body, claimed the actress, who had been married to a mob thug named Pasquale Di Cecco, was murdered, the theory most widely held in the movie colony.

*

Bridget Veronica Kelly developed a fall-guy attitude so strong that she couldn't possibly have been called anything *but* **Patsy Kelly.** She began performing by pretending to dance at home in Williamsburg, Brooklyn, although what she was really doing was tripping over the furniture. "I led with my chin, because my knees were helpless," said Kelly (1910–1981). Her parents, John and Delia from Ireland's County Mayo, enrolled her in proper lessons, yet even in class she was the patsy.

Putting her gift for throwaway lines to use, she joined comedian Frank Fay in his vaudeville act in 1926, when she was sixteen. Fay is credited with teaching her to ad lib, though he was also said to have hogged all the funny lines. As a solo on Broadway, Kelly stood out in *Earl Carroll's Sketchbook* and in *Wonder Bar* with Al Jolson, which got her noticed by Hal Roach, who brought her to Hollywood in 1933 to replace ZaSu Pitts in a series of comedies with Thelma Todd. The chemistry between the glamorous blond and the scrappy plain-jane brunette worked.

* Something the vivacious blond also did in 1931's *Monkey Business*.

Todd and Kelly swapped one-liners in some forty two-reelers, and as the decade wore on, Kelly was often cast as the sassy confidante of Alice Faye, Loretta Young, and Joan Blondell. In other features she played the streetwise Irish maid who deflated her pompous employers with a glare or, better yet, a pointed, deadpan remark.

Considered a consummate ad-libber, Kelly brightened more than fifty films in the thirties and forties, most of them comedies. These included *The Girl from Missouri, Go Into Your Dance, Every Night at Eight, Page Miss Glory, Sing, Baby, Sing, Pigskin Parade, Wake Up and Live, There Goes My Heart,* and *Topper Returns.* In the sixties she surfaced in *Please Don't Eat the Daisies,* with Doris Day, and as a very cranky devil worshiper menacing Mia Farrow in *Rosemary's Baby*—though in that last one it was hard not to be amused by her. In the seventies, she once again

Thelma Todd and Patsy Kelly (she's the one in the gorilla suit) in Bum Voyage, *a Hal Roach comedy of the early thirties. As Kelly was fond of saying, "We gotta get outta here."*

played wisecracking sidekicks and she shone in the Broadway revivals of the musicals *No, No, Nanette* and *Irene,* and won a Tony for the former. As she picked up her statuette she half-crankily told the crowd, "I think I'll go home and get drunk."

Occasionally introspective, especially after she'd been tippling, Kelly once remarked to an interviewer: "I was always around people who were too good." Remembering that Bill Tilden had once tried to teach her tennis, Eleanor Holm had instructed her in swimming, and Babe Didrikson attempted to improve her swing at golf, Kelly noted that she had finally "ended up caddying. That's the story of my life."

SCREWBALL QUEENS ESCAPE ARTISTS

Feeding fantasy-starved Depression-era audiences, Hollywood dished up suave guys—even if they were sometimes sloppily dressed newspapermen—and chic, smart-talking heiresses. These two forces of nature inevitably "met cute," sparks ignited, and voilà!: Love, commonly marred by some complications that could only be smoothed out by the final funny fade-out. The women of the screwball comedies of the thirties—played impressively by actresses who could also play drama—were confident, well-groomed, and, above all, witty, though it was frequently their refreshingly gorgeous looks that attracted the fellas to them in the first place. Everyday realities? Messages? Blue collars? Not in the black-and-white gems starring these screen goddesses—whose particular brand of escapist vehicles wound down with the outbreak of World War II.

Carole Lombard, winding up for Nothing Sacred (1937).

Carole Lombard

While Mary Astor could be counted upon to bring class and credibility to dramatic roles in the thirties, Carole Lombard brought divinity to the era's comedies. Sheathed in silks and satins and always looking as though she were late, racing downstairs to meet her chauffeur, Lombard threw wonderful movie tantrums that were staples of such charming period pieces as *Twentieth Century, My Man Godfrey,* and *Nothing Sacred.* Lombard knew her limitations as an actress, as well as the physical ones in her appearance; following reconstructive surgery after a 1925 car accident that had forever left a scar on her left cheek, she had a still photographer snap her from all angles so she could determine how best to be lit. By the late thirties Lombard was on the short list to play Scarlett O'Hara, though she smacked far more of Park Avenue than of the Old South. Still, like Margaret Mitchell's heroine in *Gone With the Wind,* Carole Lombard always seemed determined never to get old before her time.

She was seven when she arrived in Los Angeles, having been born Jane Alice Peters in Fort Wayne, Indiana, in 1908. Her brothers taught her to box and play baseball, and her divorced mother allowed her to go to drama school. In 1921 she played a tomboy in the Allan Dwan movie *A Perfect Crime,* which was all the encouragement she needed to drop out of school. By 1927 she was working in Mack Sennett comedies with the new name of Carol Lombard (the "e" in Carole came and went until she was a well-established star).

Lombard's first big hit was 1934's *Twentieth Century* with John Barrymore, in which she played the gorgeously exasperated movie star Lily Garland to his Oscar Jaffe—a washed-up stage producer and Lily's former husband. In a last-ditch effort to save his career and get his play financed, Oscar tries desperately to corral Lily into starring in his upcoming Broadway show while the two of them travel from Chicago to New York aboard the Twentieth Century Limited. From that film on, through 1937's *Nothing Sacred,* in which, as a woman who thinks she's dying, she fools a sympathetic New York with her sob story, and the classic 1942

To Be or Not to Be, co-starring Jack Benny, Carole Lombard was the queen of screwball comedy. Upon her shocking death in January of 1942 (the plane on which she was riding flew into a mountain during a war bonds tour), President Roosevelt cabled her widower, Clark Gable: "She brought joy to all who knew her, and to millions who only knew her as a great artist. . . . She is and always will be a star, one we shall never forget, nor cease to be grateful to."

Claudette Colbert

The pretentious Cecil B. DeMille may have wrapped her in a rug and unveiled her as Cleopatra, but it was the talkies' great populist director Frank Capra who knew what to do with Claudette Colbert. He cast her as the runaway heiress in *It Happened One Night,* providing her the opportunity to win an Oscar *and* to bring

Lombard between takes, on 1938's Fools for Scandal. *As magnetic offscreen as she was on, Lombard was married to the actor William Powell (her co-star in the appealing 1936* My Man Godfrey*) from 1931 to 1933. Her second husband, whom she married in 1939 before he started shooting* Gone With the Wind, *was Clark Gable, the so-called King of Hollywood. The union was known to be rocky.*

new meaning to hitchhiking. Among the movie's rich scenes: the sight of Colbert lifting her skirt above her knee and stopping a flivver dead in its tracks. The delightful comedy, in which Clark Gable played her rumpled newshound chronicler and suitor, also paved the way for Colbert, primarily a dramatic actress, to shine in such sparkling later comedy vehicles as Anatole Litvak's 1937 *Tovarich,* Ernst Lubitsch's 1938 *Bluebeard's Eight Wives,* George Cukor's 1939 *Zaza,* W. S. Van Dyke's 1939 *It's a Wonderful World,* and Preston Sturges's irrepressible 1942 *The Palm Beach Story,* wherein she leaves her dreamboat hubby, Joel McCrea, in order to save their marriage. It was also in that stylish side-splitter that she observed, "Men don't get smarter as they get older. They just lose their hair."

As for her, aging never seemed to affect her—until the end. She died in 1996, indomitable as ever, still dressing and wearing makeup for the guests at her estate in Barbados, despite a series of debilitating strokes that confined her to a wheelchair.

Myrna Loy

"Myrna Loy—what a joy!" crowed Lillian Gish at the top of her lungs in 1985 from the stage of Carnegie Hall. Loy, whose career spanned a remarkable six decades, was being saluted for her body of work, which ranged from playing exotic Asians in early Fu Manchu movies to her perfect wife and mother in Samuel Goldwyn and William Wyler's *The Best Years of Our Lives*.

But the role that made Myrna Loy a star and maybe the most beloved movie actress of the era was comedic: her sophisticated Nora Charles to debonair William Powell's Nick Charles in *The Thin Man* (M-G-M, 1934, with sequels and spin-offs to follow). He was the sly and witty detective; she, the rich, smart wife. And both of them, downing martinis straight-up at every opportunity. "Don't ask me how we did that," Loy admitted in 1987. "Neither Bill nor I drank." The movie was made on the run, with Loy's entrance—being led by Asta, the dog—a pratfall. "I was supposed to stroll in looking very chic, loaded down with packages," recalled Loy. "'Can you fall?' Woody [W. S. Van Dyke, the director] asked. 'Do you

Opposite: *The former Claudette Lily Chauchoin was born in Paris in 1905 and was brought to New York at the age of six. After high school she attended the Art Students League, hoping to become a fashion designer, but a chance meeting at a Manhattan party led to her stage debut in 1923 and then ingenue roles throughout the rest of the decade. In 1927, while still appearing on Broadway, she'd cross the 59th Street Bridge into Queens to make silent movies at the Astoria Studios. Her first major film success came in 1931,* The Smiling Lieutenant *with Maurice Chevalier, and she would never fully abandon the stage, even after she became one of Hollywood's top commodities. Here she is at but one pinnacle, with Clark Gable in* It Happened One Night.

Left: *The couple everyone adored, Nick and Nora Charles (William Powell and Myrna Loy), in 1934's* The Thin Man.

By the early thirties Metro-Goldwyn-Mayer was casting Loy—born Myrna Williams, near Helena, Montana, in 1905—in breezy but forgettable vehicles. Then came The Thin Man. *(Here she is with her co-star Asta, his stand-in, and the dog's fan mail.)* "I loved it and the prospect of a witty role," she recalled in her 1987 memoir, Myrna Loy: Being and Becoming. "I'd fired an occasional quip, but my roles had been very straight up until that point." When the movie hit she earned the nickname "the perfect wife." Offscreen, she was married four different times (her husbands included producer Arthur Hornblow, Jr., and car-rental heir John Hertz, Jr.), and, despite the "Republican" circumstances of a lot of her roles, politically she was a staunch liberal Democrat. Her support of the Free French against the Nazis won her a medal from France's President DeGaulle after the war, and she served as the United States representative to UNESCO. Myrna Loy died in 1993.

know how to fall?' I said, 'I've never worked for Mack Sennett, but I'm a dancer. I think I can do it.' . . . I must've been crazy. I could have killed myself, but my dance training paid off. I dashed in with Asta and all those packages, tripped myself, went down, slid across the floor, and hit the mark with my chin. It was absolutely incredible!"

Jean Arthur

"That voice!" Frank Capra exclaimed about Jean Arthur. "Low, husky—at times it broke pleasantly into the higher octaves like a thousand tinkling bells." So sold was the moviemaker on Arthur's pipes that he went running to Columbia Pictures' studio boss, Harry Cohn, to rave about them.

"Great voice?" replied Cohn. "D'ja see her face? Half of it's angel, and the other half horse."

Cohn was wrong. Arthur had star quality, and she is the only screwball queen never to have played an heiress. Her roles were that of the everyday "average" girl who gained audience sympathy and, with her down-to-earth nonglamorous appeal, the guy by the last reel. She first made movie audiences laugh in John Ford's 1935 *The Whole Town's Talking,* as the love object of Edward G. Robinson,

Gladys Georgiana Greene (Jean Arthur's birth name) was born in New York City in 1905 and quit school to take up modeling. She'd done a lot of work in silent western movies until she made her mark in John Ford's 1935 The Whole Town's Talking. *What Hollywood started talking about was her unique voice onscreen and her various insecurities off. She retired at age forty-eight in 1953, after co-starring with Alan Ladd in the western* Shane. *Her film just prior to that, 1948's* Foreign Affair, *was something of a nightmare for its director, Billy Wilder. During shooting, he claimed, Arthur convinced herself that the best close-ups were going to her co-star Marlene Dietrich and not to her, despite Wilder's protestations to the contrary. Finally, claimed Wilder, nearly forty-five years after the picture was made, his phone rang at home. It was Jean Arthur. She had just seen the picture on television the night before and she was calling to apologize.*

who played the dual role of a meek clerk and a bullying mobster (it was the clerk who adored Arthur). In George Stevens's 1943 *The More the Merrier,* about the wartime residential shortage in Washington, D.C., she grabbed handsome leading man Joel McCrea—though it had been under Capra's direction, playing opposite Gary Cooper and Jimmy Stewart, that she reached the peak of her popularity . . . and the leading men reached theirs. Jean Arthur took Mr. Deeds to town and chaperoned Mr. Smith around Washington.

"Jean is my favorite actress," declared Capra. "Probably because she was unique. Never have I seen a performer plagued with such a chronic case of stage jitters." Of her nerves, he said, "Those weren't butterflies in her stomach. They were wasps."

Irene Dunne

It's been said that because so many of Irene Dunne's movies were remade and the originals taken out of circulation, the contemporary public is no longer familiar with the gifted screen star. Then there are her detractors, who'd just as soon have her movies vanish. The critic James Agee, responding to the sometimes-held theory that Dunne's screwball heroines lacked Lombard's manic lunacy or Jean Arthur's sweet but palatable vulnerability, wrote, "I am not among those who take to Irene Dunne—as a rule, she makes my skin crawl."

Still, the Kentucky-born Dunne was one of the most popular stars of screwball comedy. Her original aim had been to sing opera—how better to explain that terrific musical laugh—but when New York's Metropolitan passed her over she headed full steam to Broadway, which led to Hollywood. The movies cast her in such tearjerkers as *Back Street* and *Magnificent Obsession* before letting her exercise her singing voice in *Roberta* and *Show Boat.* It was her portrayal of a small-town author in the 1936 farce *Theodora Goes Wild* that proved Dunne could tickle audiences, something she did with aplomb opposite Cary Grant in such happy romps as 1937's *The Awful Truth* and 1940's *My Favorite Wife.* "Comedy," she said, "was always very easy for me—and it's not as satisfying to me as a dramatic role. I think you give more of yourself."

Barbara Stanwyck

Think of Barbara Stanwyck as the female James Cagney: a highly versatile trouper, a performer who never bothered to worry whether a role was sympathetic (so long as it was juicy), and always a pleasure to watch. Early movie fans knew her as an everyday working girl in a broad range of roles (including the lead in the highly watchable if shameless weepy *Stella Dallas),* while to baby boomers she will forever be the strikingly handsome, white-haired matriarch of the Barkley Ranch on television's *The Big Valley* (1965–69). Stanwyck, born Ruby Stevens in Brooklyn in 1907, was orphaned by the time she was four. Forced to quit school while she was still in adolescence, she wrapped packages in a department store by age thirteen (as had the young Fanny Brice) and danced as a chorus girl by age fifteen. Gradually she worked her way up to dramatic leading roles on Broadway, and starred for nine months in the 1926 drama *The Noose.* She moved to Hollywood with her first husband, the comedian Frank Fay (whom she married in 1928 and divorced seven years later),* and her contract was shared by both Warner Bros. and Columbia Studios. C. B. DeMille, who cast her in 1939's *Union Pacific,* found her the most cooperative and least temperamental actress he ever worked with, and Frank Capra fell in love with her (she starred in his 1933 *The Bitter Tea of General Yen* and 1941's *Meet John Doe).* Three film roles stand out as her best, and two of them were comedic: the jocular 1941 *The Lady Eve* and 1942's *Ball of Fire,* and the noir-ish 1944 *Double Indemnity.* She could be smart-alecky—as in the first two—or downright treacherous, as she demonstrated to perfection in *Indemnity.* What Barbara Stanwyck couldn't be was ordinary.

Katharine Hepburn

"The script was a good one. Cary Grant was really wonderful in it. And I was good too," allowed Katharine Hepburn, with whom it was always extremely difficult to argue. "And the leopard was excellent." For the real-life Connecticut Yankee Hepburn, excellence seemed a birthright. Born rich, born bossy, born to shine, she delivered the goods throughout a career that lasted from her professional stage

The iconoclast, Katharine Hepburn, in Hollywood

debut, in 1928's *The Czarina,* to her final film (her forty-fourth), Warren Beatty's 1994 *Love Affair.*

Continuing her summation of her funniest picture and the only one, except for a pratfall in *The Philadelphia Story,* in which she attempted slapstick—*Bringing up Baby,* directed by the peerless Howard Hawks—the Great Kate said: "I didn't have enough brains to be scared, so I did a lot of scenes with the leopard just roaming around."

The plot involved the heiress Susan Vance (Hepburn), who is attracted to the paleontologist David Vance (Grant), whose dinosaur bone is stolen by the dog George (Asta) belonging to her aunt, Mrs. Elizabeth Carlton Random (May Robson). The affair is complicated by the aunt's checkbook, since the paleontologist would benefit greatly if only the grande dame would contribute to his museum. He's engaged, by the way, to a sexless creature, Virginia Walker (Alice Swallow). And everybody's life is complicated by the fact that Susan's brother has sent her a leopard.

During filming, the shot in which the cat follows Hepburn (wearing a full-length negligee) back and forth across the bedroom of her Park Avenue apartment while she is on the phone to Grant went smoothly. The next did not. Her skirt had metal tabs

* Her second husband, to whom she was married from 1939 to 1952, was the actor Robert Taylor.

espite its high register on the laugh meter and its subsequent reputation thanks to TV showings, the 1938 *Bringing Up Baby* was a box-office failure in its day and followed a string of Hepburn duds because audiences were turned off by her society-girl screen persona. She'd soon bounce back—and prove her gift for comedy—in the deftly grand *Holiday* and *The Philadelphia Story.* Continuing her successful roll, she would be paired with Spencer Tracy, often for witty battles of the sexes. *Woman of the Year* (she's an internationally renowned political commentator, he's a sports columnist), *Adam's Rib* (they're husband-and-wife lawyers on opposing sides of a case in which a woman took a potshot at her louse of a spouse), and *Pat and Mike* (she's an athlete, he's her manager) were their best. Hepburn displayed an ironic wit as the weary yet still-feisty matriarch Eleanor of Aquitaine in the 1968 historical drama *The Lion in Winter.* Surrounded by treacheries, infidelities, and murder, and facing imprisonment by her royal husband, Eleanor blithely muses: "Well, what family doesn't have its ups and downs?"

Hepburn's best moment in Baby: *not with the cat, but with the dog, George. When Cary Grant whistles for the fox terrier, Kate suggests: "Don't do that. He knows you want him and he'll hide."*

What every Park Avenue apartment needs: a leopard, or so was the case in Bringing Up Baby, *1938.*

at its hem, to make the garment "swing prettily. But—a large *but*—one quick swirl and that leopard made a spring for my back," she said. Thereafter, the beast was confined by a leash.

GERTRUDE BERG
BRONX CHEER

When Hollywood screenwriter Leonard Spigelgass was casting the lead for his 1959 Broadway comedy *A Majority of One,* about a widowed Bronx Yiddishe Mama who accompanies her assimilated American-corporate-life executive son to Japan, he balked when his producers suggested Gertrude Berg. To the playwright, Berg, whose comic radio trademark was fractured English and sing-song delivery of "Yoo hoo, Mrs. Bloom" (called to summon her neighbor out the back kitchen window of her New York "apahtment"), represented all the Jewish stereotypes* that got under *his* skin.

But given Berg's possibility as a box-office draw, Spigelgass condescended to meet her. "She showed up," he recalled, "and I'll never forget her entrance." Rather than wearing a kitchen apron, which was the image the writer had of her in his mind, "Gertrude came dressed impeccably, with a mink coat. She was a lady head to toe."

She ended up capturing not only the role, but also a Tony for her performance opposite Sir Cedric Hardwicke, and Spigelgass's eternal admiration: "When, opening night, she made her entrance with a kimono incongruously wrapped around her round little figure," he remembered, "she did something subtle and brilliant that wasn't in the script. She gave this little shrug and looked up to heaven. It brought down the house."

Brilliant and subtle *was* Gertrude Berg (1899–1966), to say nothing of prolific. Within the realm of American dialect comedy—given *Life with Luigi* (American-Italian), *Duffy's Tavern* (Irish-American), *I Remember Mama* (Swedish-American),

"If it's nobody, I'll call back," Berg instructed family members in her sing-song voice whenever the phone rang. (Yiddish, per se, was not spoken on the show.) Other Molly-isms: "Enter, whoever"; "It's late, Jake, time to expire"; "We're at the crossroads and the parting of the ways." The Goldbergs cast, posing at the network studio in 1931, played out the household doings of matriarchal Molly (Gertrude Berg), her tailor-husband Jake (James Watters), children Rosalie (Roslyn Silber) and Sammy (Alfred Corn), and Uncle David (not shown), who was Molly's brother.

* The comic playwright-screenwriter Paul Rudnick, taking his cues from the author Philip Roth, once described the Jewish mother as "monstrous, a castrating ogress bearing waxed fruit, blintzes, and mutation mink."

Once widowed and thrice-divorced, Hattie McDaniel (1898–1952) starred as TV's Beulah (here with co-star Henry Blair, for a 1949 Halloween episode). The actress ended her years at the Motion Picture Country House in California's San Fernando Valley. Her Gone With the Wind *Oscar had already been donated to Howard University in Washington, D.C.*

Sophie Tucker." Still, McDaniel found it difficult making ends meet. When she was finally hired for a 1929 touring production of *Show Boat,* she'd already worked as a ladies' room attendant.

In Hollywood, that was the role she usually played. Yet, in her way, McDaniel was a revolutionary: the first African-American woman to sing on American radio, the first to win an Academy Award (for *Gone With the Wind),* the first to star in her own series—*Beulah,* initially on radio, then on television. She rolled with the punches on radio's *Amos 'n' Andy* and *The Eddie Cantor Show,* but it was in her movie roles—yes, as the hired black maid—that she displayed her gift for brilliant comic understatement. She laughed out loud on-screen in response to Mae West's ordering her to "Beulah . . . peel me a grape," and she really shone at getting Scarlett O'Hara's goat. When Scarlett announces that she has no intention of eating her lunch, because she's saving her appetite to eat in front of her beau Ashley Wilkes (who claims to like a girl with a healthy appetite), McDaniel's Mammy tells her headstrong mistress, "What a gentleman says and what they thinks is two different things. And I ain't noticing Mister Ashley asking for to marry you." Talk about having the last laugh.

TALLULAH BANKHEAD
THE UNINHIBITED

So many marvelous yarns exist about Tallulah Bankhead (1903–1968) that it would be a crime to discount any as apocryphal. Take the instance when she was supposedly shown to her suite at the George V—some versions purport it was the Ritz—and the bellhop reported, "Miss Bankhead, this is where the Duke and Duchess of Windsor spent their honeymoon." "Ah yes," responded Bankhead, placing her hand on the bed. "It's still cold." Or the so-called time she was in the ladies' room and bellowed out to the woman in the adjoining stall: "Dahling, sorry to bother you at a time like this, but would there happen to be any toilet paper in there?"

"Why, I'm afraid not," came the sheepish reply.

"Well, dahling," pressed Tallulah, "have you any Kleenex in your purse?"

After a pause, again a timid, "Sorry, no."

"Well," replied Tallulah, "would you happen to have two fives for a ten?"

Not bad for a convent-educated girl and the daughter of the Speaker of the House of Representatives, William Brockman Bankhead (Democrat–Alabama). Tallulah Bankhead—first name Indian, the second Scottish—delivered brilliant stage performances in London and New York (*The Little Foxes, The Skin of Our Teeth, Private Lives*) and some memorable ones on screen (*Lifeboat*), though her celebrated reputation came not only from her acting but perhaps primarily from her tempestuous disposition, outspokenness, and ribald sense of humor.

"I have tried several varieties of sex," she is quoted as having said. "The conventional position makes me claustrophobic. And the others either give me a stiff neck or lockjaw." Never was she above self-parody, drawling her trademark "hello, daaaaaaaahling" on many a radio broadcast (including a show of her own) and on

> "An onion can make you cry, but show me the vegetable that can make you laugh!"
> —Tallulah Bankhead

Tallulah Bankhead's reputation for outrageousness frequently outdistanced her career achievements. Here she and Agnes Moorehead (left) surface in the 1953 Main Street to Broadway, *a trifle of a movie about the Great White Way.*

the very funniest of TV's *The Lucy-Desi Comedy Hour* episodes, 1957's "The Celebrity Next Door."

TALLULAH (slamming the door on Lucy)**:** . . . you do a revolting imitation of me!
LUCY: So do you!

Seldom without a cigarette and drink—the aftereffects of the former caused her to be called, justifiably, "the Alabama Foghorn"—Tallulah enjoyed appetites as towering as her anecdotes. "Cocaine isn't habit-forming," she declared. "I should know, I've been using it for years." Asked how on earth she could have performed oral sex on one of the ugliest men in New York, Tallulah supposedly replied: "Dahling, anything to get away from that face."

Though she was married—for a time—to the actor John Emery, she was rumored to have had innumerable lovers of both sexes. Yet for all her experience and worldly sophistication, Tallulah Bankhead—actress, raconteur, politician's daughter, bridge fanatic, Vietnam pacifist—claimed there were really only five geniuses in the world: Willie Mays and the Four Marx Brothers.

MARTHA RAYE
INDESTRUCTIBLE

With legs like Tina Turner's, a mouth like an air-raid siren, and lungs like Tarzan's, Martha Raye couldn't help but stand out among great women of comedy. It wasn't simply that she could *look* funny, she could *act* funny—and did, in a lengthy if bumpy career that stretched from vaudeville to videos.

She was born Margaret Theresa Yvonne Reed on August 27, 1916, in the charity ward of a hospital in Butte, Montana. Her singer-dancer parents, Pete and Peggy Reed, were Irish immigrants who traveled the U.S. carnival circuit. "I didn't work until I was three," said Martha, who, when she grew older, picked her stage name out of a Manhattan phone directory. "But after that, I never stopped."

Her mother taught her to read and write while the family, which also included Martha's sister and brother, crisscrossed the country. Only occasionally did young Martha attend school. "Our home was in an old, broken-down Pierce Arrow auto which my father drove," she recalled. "We put the scenery in the back seat and that was where we slept at night. We cooked on Sterno. And we went from town to town, looking for bookings." Reassessing those times, she said, "I thought I was having a wonderful life. I never realized I was being culturally deprived, that I was having a lousy upbringing. We were too busy making a living to worry about stuff like that."

> "Ask any girl what she'd rather be than beautiful, and she'll say more beautiful."
> —Martha Raye

Rather than taking the obvious career path by pursuing musical comedy roles on stage, Raye opted to try comedy routines and novelty songs in clubs. By age fifteen, she was singing, dancing, and mugging in a comedy act for children—and making ends meet by working as a hospital nurse's aide. Soon she began piling up credits in adult Broadway revues, including *Earl Carroll's Sketchbook,* and appearing on the radio with Al Jolson and Bob Hope.

She moved to Hollywood, where she became one of the circle of entertainers who regularly performed on Sunday nights at the Trocadero. Funnymen Jimmy Durante and Joe E. Lewis were playing her straightmen the night producer Norman Taurog dropped in, and he had Paramount hire her to co-star with Bing Crosby in the 1936 Paramount film *Rhythm on the Range.* Doing a slapstick drunk scene and delivering a song called "Mr. Paganini," she became a star overnight—and was signed to a five-year studio contract.

Bright as the ending to that chapter of the story should have been, Martha Raye didn't exactly fit into the studio system. She could take on roles that were romantic and alluring or she could play an overly aggressive man-chaser. She could never be typed. "They tried to make a glamour girl out of me," Raye said of the studio executives. "Let's face it, I'm not a glamour girl. I'm a clown."

During World War II, Raye found her true calling: entertaining troops. Her U.S.O. tour of bases in England and Africa with Kay Francis, Carole Landis, and Mitzi Mayfair inspired the 1944 film *Four Jills in a Jeep.* Raye continued to boost troop morale throughout both the Korean and Vietnam wars, and received two Purple Hearts for endangering her own life as she reached out to soldiers. "They ask so little and give so much," Raye said of the young American fighters in Vietnam. "The least we can do back home here is give them the love, the respect, and the dignity that they, our flag, and our country deserve."*

Raye's most priceless bit of film work was inarguably her performance in Charlie Chaplin's 1947 *Monsieur Verdoux,* as Annabella Bonheur, the loud-mouthed, nouveau-riche object of Chaplin's affection. Well, actually, it's her money he adores. No matter how Chaplin's Bluebeard character tries to kill Annabella, he simply can't, not even when he takes her out on a lonely lake in a rowboat. The result was hilarious, even if their styles are worlds apart—he's refined, she plays broad. "Do you know," Raye recalled in 1972, "that when Chaplin called to offer me the part, I hung up on him. I thought it was a joke."

Her personal life, on the other hand, was anything but funny. "As an entertainer, she's a genius," a colleague once said. "Socially, she's completely unsure of herself." Raye blamed her unsettled childhood for a lot of her misery, saying, "I

After a spasmodic movie career, Martha Raye hit a certain stride on television. Milton Berle gave her a start on the small screen, and by 1954 she had appeared on nearly all the variety and comedy shows, including frequent spots on *The Red Skelton Show* (where her ex-husband David Rose conducted the program's orchestra). Still ahead would be successful bookings in nightclubs, cabaret, and theater. In the seventies, she appeared on TV's *McMillan and Wife* (taking over for Nancy Walker) and on the sitcom *Alice,* as the mother of the Vic Tayback character. Still, most fans by then knew her primarily as the lady with the big mouth who appeared on Polident denture-cleaner commercials.

* In 1992, Raye unsuccessfully sued the producers of the 1991 Bette Midler film *For the Boys* for basing the script on her life. Though there were similarities between Raye and Midler's screen character, the movie protagonist was an amalgam of many entertainers, including Sophie Tucker.

riage, and my career stopped. I don't eve
backed away from them. When things we
have any part of my trouble. I think thing
not old. I'm old enough, but I photograph
lic. I still get fan mail. I don't know where
where I'm going. I would just like to be h

grew up insecure, with no home ties, and maybe that's why I'll always be insecure and worried about finding happiness."

She had six husbands: the makeup artist Buddy Westmore, the composer David Rose, the businessman Neal Lang, the dancers Nick Condos (by whom she had a daughter, Melody) and Edward Begley, and the policeman Robert O'Shea. (He had been her bodyguard, and Raye paid the former Mrs. O'Shea $20,000 for the alienation of her husband's affections. Despite the investment, the Raye-O'Shea

"I know I've got a big mouth," said Martha Raye, posing with a simian friend for a Paramount publicity shot. "I guess I've won a lot of fans by stretching it to make it look even bigger than it is. That's swell and I'm grateful. You're lucky in this business if people like you for any reason."

guest on Rudy Vallee's progran
lar, performing song parodies ar
took off for the service in 1943,
able to command a $1-million-a-
of her years in the medium. "It w

Clearly, radio was her forte,
but most notably Burns and Allen
small screen in the early fifties. Nc
ger; NBC's *I Married Joan* gave her
Joan fashion, she built her own bac
ring somewhere in the mortar—anc
who, if they pressed their memory t
theme song:

> *I Married Joan*
> *What a girl, what a whirl, what a*

IMOGENE COCA
CAESAR'S CLEOPATRA

elevision's first elfin comic—who wa
was Imogene Coca. In 1949 she appe
live, ninety-minute Saturday night prog.
the show changed sponsors* it also change
renamed *Your Show of Shows*. Not that the
hilarious.

With remarkable dexterity, Coca r
Caesar, gesture for gesture, playing
woman he would meet in the stree
legendary writers who included La
and Woody Allen, Coca—as the or
ble guest star—got to play Jane to Cae
Caesar's *From Here to Eternity* Burt Lanc
Caesar's Charlie Hickenlooper, a hopeless
was said of Ginger Rogers in her partners
Sid Caesar did Imogene Coca had to do . .
Or, in Coca's case, sometimes in army boots.
blissful comic union had to do with their salarie
week, Coca $10,000.

*Who carried whom? Critics long
ago declared Sid Caesar and
Imogene Coca equals.*

* Admiral was a manufacturer of television sets, but the show proved so popula
met and the company was forced to withdraw its sponsorship of the program.

BETTY
THE C

oiste
bers
the f
war years,
laughing o
Born
as a child
thirteen sh
the Vincen
Miller.) Hu
Bombshell
her the fol
she made
Sturges's f
the eager
came whe
the 1950 r
not a Garla
the role he
atop a cha
her back a
1952 *The*
walked ou
her second
downward
Short
was fired a
well. After
panion) dy
"personal
bankruptcy
"I'm s
lost my mc

union laste
year-old M
ager. Raye
died three

n worldwide bulletin-worthy news, Ball died on April 26,
1989. The day afterward, the Museum of Broadcasting
(since renamed the Museum of Radio and Television) in
New York set up television monitors in an abandoned store-
front on Fifth Avenue. On several screens behind the glass,
passersby could glimpse (but not hear) snippets from the
old *I Love Lucy*: Lucy stomping grapes, Lucy holding up a
magic-potion bottle labeled "Vitameatavegemin," Lucy pop-
ping up inside a deep freezer with icicles on her eyelashes,
Lucy being pinned against her kitchen sink by a hyperglan-
dular loaf of bread from the oven (to which she had added
too much yeast), Lucy—with Ethel—trying to keep up with
a conveyer belt in a chocolate factory, and Lucy being
kissed by Desi/Ricky as the TV screen faded into a giant,
framed heart. There wasn't a dry eye in the crowd.

motion pictures passes all underst
ing anywhere except Hollywood."*

And yet it was as the successor
to the most cosmopolitan funny lady of
them all that Lucy aspired to be. "I
admired Carole Lombard from the word
go," Lucy admitted, "every suit she
wore, every time I saw her hair—I
loved her." Yet the movie studios didn't
use Lucy, a former hat model, for
sophisticated comedy; they relegated
her to roles as a glamorous extra. "I
never much cared for myself in
movies," she said years after television
had made her a pop culture icon, "but
I remember when I was first shown
television. I thought, 'Now this is something I could get into.'"

Quite the understatement. At the
show's peak, *Lucy* played to ten million
viewers a week, at a time when there were only fifteen million television sets in
the country. On January 19, 1953, more people watched the birth of the Ricardos'
son, "Little Ricky," than had watched Queen Elizabeth's coronation or President
Eisenhower's inauguration. In 1952, Democratic presidential candidate Adlai
Stevenson pre-empted *I Love Lucy*. Read but one piece of the hate mail that flood-
ed into the mailboxes of the candidate and of CBS: "I love Lucy. I like Ike. Drop
dead."

Volumes have been produced on Lucy's greatest moments on her original
series (the later *The Lucy Show* and *Here's Lucy* offered only occasional pleasures
which were more often than not tarnished rehashes of the golden moments she
had achieved the first time out). But words pale in comparison to her actions. She
was a balletic as Chaplin, also as vulnerable, to the point that if she had come
along first, we no doubt would be comparing him to her. She was as lightning-
quick as any of the Marx Brothers, but unlike them (dirty old men, one and all),
she was a striking beauty. Her distinct comic persona was as finely honed as Jack
Benny's vainglorious pennypincher and W. C. Fields's gin-soaked misanthrope (or
Will Rogers's folksy cowboy, for that matter), and the love the public harbored for
her outweighed even the overwhelming affection it felt for Bob Hope—whose
admirable if sometimes boastful comedy could nevertheless leave his listener fee

* Critics never stopped loving Lucy. As Tom Shales wrote in the *Washington Post* on August 26, 1997: "The fifties are a much
maligned decade, often called culturally bland and repressed. . . . But if we had Joe McCarthy and polio and the Checkers Sp
and millions of cigarette smokers, we also had food that was safe to eat and water that was safe to drink and television that
safe to watch. And we had *Lucy*. And we are oh so lucky to have her forever. She was the greatest star, and this was the gr
show."

ing cold. Indeed, try to imagine television, or the cultural landscape, without its beloved dizzy redhead.

Sorry, not a funny proposition.

JUDY HOLLIDAY
SMART BLONDE

"**D**o me a favor, will ya, Harry? Drop dead." If she had never said another word, Judy Holliday, who delivered this bit of advice to her bully of a benefactor in Garson Kanin's *Born Yesterday,* would have achieved stage and screen immortality. All right, she was pretty hot stuff in the Spencer Tracy–Katharine Hepburn sparring match *Adam's Rib,* playing the trigger-happy cheated-upon wife who takes well-deserved aim at her husband (Tom Ewell). And how

As the switchboard-operator and master meddler Ella Peterson in the 1960 film Bells Are Ringing, *based on her 1956 Broadway hit, the superb Judy Holliday delivered her thirteenth and final film performance. Fielding calls with her is the answering service's daffy owner, played by Jean Stapleton (sitting), who eleven years later started playing Edith Bunker to comic perfection on television's* All in the Family.

about that final number of hers in the musical *Bells Are Ringing,* "I'm Going Back"? Mocking Al Jolson and yet creating her own catchphrase, she dreams of returning to work at the Bonjour Tristesse Brassiere Company and she interjects: "Send me my mail there!" In a word, great. Other words: Intelligent. Intuitive. Musical, nearly to the point of being operatic in her deft comic delivery and multitude of voices. And totally New York. Some other Holliday tips: Born Judith Tuvim (Hebrew for "holiday"), in 1922. Started backstage at the switchboard of Orson Welles's Mercury Theater. Made her debut (in 1939) at the Village Vanguard as one of the Revuers, a group that also included performer-writers Betty Comden and Adolph Green, who would later write the book and lyrics to *Bells Are Ringing,* among other shows and movies. Landed the role of *Born Yesterday*'s dumb blond Billie ("I never say 'ain't,' didja notice? Since I was very small I never said it") when Jean Arthur dropped out on the road, then made the 1950 movie version—which Arthur also dropped out of—and in doing so nabbed the Oscar away from such competition as Bette Davis's Margo Channing and Gloria Swanson's Norma Desmond. To repeat, she

was great. Make that GREAT. And tragic. Dead at age forty-three, in 1965, from cancer. But to hear her say to William Holden in *Born Yesterday,* using one of the many voice inflections for which she was famous, "Lemme ask ya something. Are you one of those talkers, or would you be interested in a little action?"

EVE ARDEN
ARCH SUPPORT

After Our Miss Brooks *left the air in 1957, Arden (shown here with Brooks's gruff principal, played by Gale Gordon) starred as a traveling lecturer on* The Eve Arden Show *(1957–58) and then as a meddling relative on* The Mothers-in-Law *(1967–69). For the 1978 movie musical* Grease, *she got to play the principal. In the late eighties Woody Allen wanted her for one of his films, but by then she was tending to her dying husband, the actor Brooks West. Said Kaye Ballard, the co-star of* The Mothers-in-Law, *of Arden: "She had an air of sophistication, class, and wit. She was ladylike even doing a pratfall."*

When the Desilu sitcom *Our Miss Brooks,* which had been a radio program since 1948, moved to television in 1953, the still-fledgling medium got its first "career-girl" heroine. Constance Brooks, as memorably played by Eve Arden, was a winsome maiden English teacher at Madison High School, where she was the apple of her student Walter Denton's eye (Walter was Richard Crenna), though her affections leaned toward Madison's diffident biology teacher Philip Boynton (Robert Rockwell, in a role played by Jeff Chandler on radio). Miss Brooks's free spirit—this was back in the days when teachers were educators and not prison wardens—never quite meshed with the manner of the school's stern principal, Osgood Conklin (Gale Gordon), though Conklin's daughter Harriet adored Miss Brooks. Harriet had company.

ANN SOTHERN
PROFESSIONAL POLISH

While Miss Brooks taught English on *Our Miss Brooks,* another careerist, Susie McNamara, took dictation from her boss, New York theatrical agent Peter Sands (Don Porter), on the 1953–57 *Private Secretary. Susie,* as the show was also known, brought the talents of Ann Sothern to the small screen, thus providing viewers with a popular, plucky bachelor girl until *The Mary Tyler Moore Show* came along.* While the fifties' glass ceiling may have kept a lid on Susie's climb up the professional ladder, she was clearly executive material, exerting the upper hand in nearly every situation and protectively arming herself with an always-snappy retort. She also proved the old Dorothy Parker adage wrong: On *Private Secretary,* men did make passes at a girl who wore glasses.

Sothern, born Harriette Lake in 1909, was a seasoned concert singer who appeared under her real name in early Warner Bros. talkies, though she made her real name—or rather, the name of Ann Sothern—in the "Maisie" B-movie series for M-G-M, in which she played the good-hearted, independent heroine in ten comedy-adventures from 1939 until 1947. (CBS also ran a Maisie radio series with Sothern from 1945 to 1952.) "My bag doesn't want to be picked up and neither do I," said Maisie, always a good girl. As for her escapades, the movie titles tell it all: *Maisie Gets Her Man, Maisie Goes to Reno,* and *Undercover Maisie*—though fans insist *Congo Maisie* was her best.

* There would be Marlo Thomas in *That Girl* (1966–1971), but sugary storylines and an overutilized laugh track do not a funny lady make.

Ann Sothern, in her Susie McNamara Private Secretary *phase. TV viewers also knew her as the voice of* My Mother, the Car *(1965–66) and as Lucille Carmichael's friend, "The Countess," on* The Lucy Show. *Movie fans last had the chance to see her in 1987's* The Whales of August. *As she told* New York Times *interviewer Aljean Harmetz when that movie came out: "I've done everything but play rodeos."*

"We'd been on TV only a few weeks when I was being deluged with fan mail from teachers and asked to address teachers' meetings," Arden (1912–1990) recalled for her 1985 memoir, *The Three Phases of Eve.* "It seemed the teachers had taken Connie Brooks to their bosoms, and the public was not far behind."

Behind the proper schoolmarmish behavior, Miss Brooks exuded a libidinous nature that she not-so-carefully concealed behind her wisecracking facade. Of Mr. Boynton, Miss Brooks once groused: "Maybe I could dump a bowl of rice over my head and whistle 'The Wedding March.'" That type of remark was a natural extension of the unsentimental lines Arden had been delivering in movies since the thirties. "I was always the girlfriend of the heroine," she said of the typecasting. Hers was the most acerbic tongue in that hen-clacking rooming house occupied by Katharine Hepburn, Ginger Rogers, Lucille Ball, and others in *Stage Door* (1937), while in the popular 1944 musical *Cover Girl,* Rita Hayworth landed on the front page of the magazine despite Arden's funny objections (Eve played the assistant to the publisher). But the wisecrack that defined the screen persona of the former Eunice Quedens of Mill Valley, California, who arrived at her stage name by joining the name of the first woman in the Bible (which happened to be the book she was reading at the time) with that of cosmetics queen Elizabeth Arden, was when she told Joan Crawford in 1945's *Mildred Pierce:* "Alligators have the right idea. They eat their young."

ROSALIND RUSSELL
FAVORITE RELATIVE

Breezing down the staircase of her swank Beekman Place duplex, shaking hands with a pet monkey perched on a cocktail-party guest's shoulder, then embracing all of humanity (save for its bigots). Rosalind Russell's Auntie Mame was the distant relative everyone wanted but seldom ever had. It wasn't just that she changed her wardrobe and her apartment's interior design every time the whim hit her, or that she had interesting friends (Mahatma Gandhi, Winston Churchill, and the dipsomaniac first lady of the American theater, Vera Charles), but in every respect (sex, travel, drink) Mame Dennis Burnside lived, lived, lived.

Russell (1908–1976), a Connecticut Yankee of the same ilk as her contemporary Katharine Hepburn, was educated at Barnard College in New York before she made a beeline from summer stock to Broadway and then to Hollywood. Comedy was not her game until director George Cukor cast her as Sylvia Fowler, the snoopiest of the dames in the 1939 bitch-a-thon *The Women,* where she elicited guffaws just by wearing the ridiculous outfits fashioned for her

Graham Greene had his Aunt Augusta, Andy Griffith his Aunt Bea, and the rest of the world its Auntie Mame. In real life, as the wife of the producer Frederick Brisson, Rosalind Russell was a very social hostess in Beverly Hills. Here she literally kicks up her heels outside her London hotel, looking very much like Mrs. Mame Dennis Burnside of Beekman Place, New York.

The one, the only, Auntie Mame— Rosalind Russell. In 1966, the musical Mame arrived on Broadway, watering down the humor but making a stage star of Angela Lansbury. Lucille Ball starred in the 1974 movie musical version, which was a botch, and in 1999 there was talk of Brbra Streisand producing the property for television.

by M-G-M wardrobe warden Adrian. (Roz's threads got dusty when she and Paulette Goddard exchanged fisticuffs in the dirt at a Reno dude ranch for divorcees-in-waiting.)

By the forties Russell was playing crisp New York career women forced to decide between keeping their jobs or marrying Brian Aherne (see *Hired Wife*, 1940). Generally, Aherne got the better of the deal: His job never came into question, and he got to keep Russell. (Came the time of Women's Liberation, Russell looked back and said she probably should have kept her job, too—*and* Aherne.) Besides Paulette Goddard, Russell's greatest sparring partner was Cary Grant in the frantically funny 1940 *His Girl Friday,* a battle-of-the-sexes reworking of the classic Ben Hecht–Charles MacArthur farce *The Front Page.* As ace reporter Hildy Johnson, Russell showed her passion for her profession and for demanding equal rights for the sexes. She was also no slouch as the fictionalized version of the *New Yorker* writer Ruth McKenney in 1942's *My Sister Eileen,* which later became the 1953 Russell Broadway musical vehicle *Wonderful Town.* But it was as novelist Patrick Dennis's free-wheeling Auntie Mame, which Russell (basing the character on her mother-in-law) claimed to have shaped herself in marathon late-night writing sessions with the play's director, Morton DaCosta, that keeps her alive in the memory of most. "Life is a banquet," declared Roz in the hit 1956 Broadway version (Hollywood's slightly sanitized yet faithful adaptation followed two years later), "and most poor sons-of-bitches are starving to death."

BELLE BARTH
BLUE BELLE

If a heckler interrupted Bette Midler during her seventies *"Clams on the Half-Shell" Revue,* she'd generally snap back: "Belle Barth used to say, 'Shut your hole, honey. Mine's makin' money.'" The line generally proved effective: the audience broke up, and the heckler ceased and desisted. That left the rest of us begging only one question:

Who was Belle Barth?

Born Annabelle Salzmann in 1911 and properly educated at Manhattan's Julia Richmond High School (later the alma mater to both Judy Holliday and Lauren Bacall), Barth took her surname from her husband. Well, one of them. She had five. During thirties vaudeville she imitated her idol Sophie Tucker, whom she physically came to resemble, though Barth would finally make a name for herself in the fifties and early sixties for her trademark blue humor.

"My next story is a little risqué," she'd daintily pretend before launching into the type of material that some, including the cops who'd bust her on obscenity charges, found better suited to rest room walls.

Vintage Barth:

> *The farmer in the dell*
> *The farmer in the dell*
> *I had a cherry once*
> *But now it's shot to hell*

Hers was the Miami-Vegas circuit, though she did play Carnegie Hall, which proved a less-than-perfect venue. Toning down her act because, as she noted from the stage, there was "fuzz" in the house, Barth turned off the crowd who'd come to hear her customary brand of forthright naughtiness. Usually she was busted when she got too liquored up to curb her tongue, or when she feared she was losing the audience's attention.

As opposed to the dogmatic Lenny Bruce, who was born later but died earlier, Barth was no First Amendment groundbreaker. She was simply good at telling dirty jokes. To quote one of her throwaway lines, "I felt as happy as the girl who got raped on Essex Street and thought it was Grand."

Of her ten minor-label record albums, the title of her first one summed her up best: *If I Embarrass You, Tell Your Friends.* Barth died of cancer in 1971.

Barth claimed to have joined the WACs during World War II. "But I had my disappointments in the service," she said. "I found out that a twenty-one-inch Admiral was only a television set."

JACKIE "MOMS" MABLEY
YOUNG AT HEART

Her housedress looked like a potato sack, her brimless hat pulled down over her ears looked like a sailor's cap turned inside out, and her often foul mouth looked to be missing all of its teeth. But what spewed forth from the gums of Jackie "Moms" Mabley (1894–1975) was often pure gold—at least, as much of it that could be distinguished. One directive from this ribald raconteur, however, came though loud and clear: "The only thing an old man can bring me," insisted Moms, "is a message from a young man."

Of her beginnings, "I was pretty," said Moms (real name: Loretta Mary Aiken, from Brevard, North Carolina), "but didn't want to become a prostitute, so I chose show business." She had no parents to speak of, given that her fireman father was

killed in the line of duty and her mother was fatally struck by a truck while return-ing from Christmas church services. While still in her teens Moms became a mom twice—both times after she'd been raped. Both children were put up for adoption.

She took her stage name from the man said to be the true love of her life, Jack Mabley, then went to work on the black vaudeville circuit, the Theater Owners Booking Association, or TOBA (said to be an acronym for Tough on Black Asses). She played Harlem's Cotton Club in 1923 and the Apollo Theater in 1939 as one of the first female comics to play the latter venue. "A woman is a woman until the day she dies," she'd tell her audiences. "But a man's a man only as long as he can!" Complaining about her (fictitious) late husband, she'd wail, "He was oooooooooooold. Mmm. He was older than dirt." Her stage character—essentially that of a dirty old woman—was based on her grandmother, a role Moms played since nearly the start of her career. "I got old when I was twenty," she would say.

Moms made her TV debut in 1967 on a Harry Belafonte special, then regu-larly surfaced on the variety and talk shows hosted by Flip Wilson, Bill Cosby, the Smothers Brothers, Mike Douglas, and Merv Griffin, where she specialized in out-raging the audience. "People love me," she told Merv. "Why, they compare me to Roy Rogers's beloved ol' horse. When I walk down the street, I hear people shout, 'Hey, Trigger! Hey, Trigger!'"

Pause.

"At least that's what I think they say."

MINNIE PEARL
COUNTRY CHARM

"How-dee! I'm just proud to be here!" Only one performer could be shouting such a salutation: Minnie Pearl, a familiar figure at The Grand Ole Opry for more than half a century and to television audiences starting in the fifties (until she was felled by a stroke in 1991; she died in Nashville five years later).

Minnie, whose real name was Sarah Ophelia Colley Cannon, created her classic backwoods character, the spinster Cousin Minnie Pearl, in the thirties. Minnie's outfit never changed: a flowered straw hat with its $1.98 price tag attached, a thrift-shop cotton-print dress, and a wicker picnic basket for a purse. Minnie earned her belly laughs from audiences by telling groaners so corny that few other comics could have gotten away with them. Most revolved around the means of "catchin' a feller" in her fictional rural home of Grinder's Switch, a name she took from a railroad crossing three miles from where she'd actually grown up.

"I'm in love!" she declared in a later routine. "I'm in love with Pee-Wee Herman! He called me a breath of spring! Well, he didn't use them words. He said I looked like the end of a hard winter!"

Opposite: *The many faces of Moms Mabley. She also had a hit record shortly after Bobby Kennedy was killed, "Abraham, Martin, and John," a memorial to assassinated political martyrs Lincoln, King, and Kennedy. At Moms's own funeral, in 1975, comedian Dick Gregory, noting how her career had blossomed late, said, "Had she been white, she would have been known fifty years ago."*

JUDY CANOVA
HOLLYWOOD HILLBILLY

What Minnie Pearl was to the Grand Ole Opry, Judy Canova (1916–1983) was to B-movies. A country-bumpkin comedienne born in Florida and reared in the hills of Georgia, Canova began her career singing hillbilly songs on the radio with her mother and brother Jake, who called themselves The Canova Cracker Trio. Next she teamed with her sister Annie and the duet became The Happiness Girls. Their act consisted of singing, yodeling, and playing the "gittar," with Judy wearing her hair in braids, crowning her head with a straw hat, and

toting a battered suitcase in her hand. The two sisters often appeared on Rudy Vallee's radio program, though slowly Judy began emerging as a solo. She did a 1935 Hollywood film (*In Caliente,* in which she mugged as Wini Shaw sang her way through the song "The Lady in Red"), and appeared in Broadway's *Ziegfeld Follies of 1936,* before Republic began producing her movies in 1940. Typical was the scene of her scrubbing floors by attaching brushes to the bottoms of her roller skates. Besides becoming that studio's top female star, she premiered *The Judy Canova Show* on NBC Radio in 1943 (it ran for a dozen years). One of her on-air gags, delivered in May of 1946, proved to be the most popular comedy routine in a poll of radio listeners. Fed the line, "One of my ancestors was a Knight of the Royal Order of the Bath—or don't you know the Order of the Bath?" Judy responded, "Why, shore—on Saturday night it was Paw first and then all the kids in the order of their ages."

In real life, Minnie Pearl, born in 1912, was no hayseed. The daughter of a well-to-do Tennessee businessman, she aspired to be an actress and dancer, and she attended Ward-Belmont College, a fashionable finishing school in Nashville. After graduation, she taught dance before being hired as a drama coach for the Wayne P. Sewall Producing Company, a small Atlanta theatrical organization that oversaw amateur stage productions in local schools around the South. She found the inspiration for her stage character in Baileyton, Alabama, when she stayed with

"Minnie Pearl is uncomplicated," said her creator. "She's apple pie and clothes dried in the sun and the smell of fresh bread baking. I don't think people think of her so much as a show business act as a friend. When I'm on stage, I'm just plain Minnie Pearl wearing my battered old straw hat and battered shoes. The price tag on my hat seems to be symbolic of all human frailty. There's old Minnie Pearl standing on stage in her best dress, telling everyone how proud she is to be there."

gave her
Berlin ga
tainment
the only
blared to

obviously flowed through her veins, and she would have other wives in hysterics over her one-liners at the laundromat. "I finally found out how my neighbor—who I call Mrs. Clean—gets her laundry so much whiter looking than mine," she'd say. "She washes it."

In 1959 Bob Hope saw her perform in San Francisco, though she bombed the particular night he was in the room. Even so, she said, "he saw courage." She credits him with giving her the self-esteem to continue, simply by his having said, "You are great."

By the sixties, critics were concurring. Her drag consisted of a fright wig ("I comb my hair with an electric toothbrush"), garish, short clothes, gloves, and a long cigarette holder—which she eventually discarded after she developed bursitis from holding it. Her movies *(Boy, Did I Get a Wrong Number* and *Did You Hear the One About the Traveling Saleslady?)* missed their marks, and her 1966 ABC TV sitcom, *The Pruitts of Southampton—* based on a Patrick Dennis novel about a wealthy family that loses its money but must maintain appearances so as not to send a shockwave through the American economy—floundered. But in nightclubs Diller soared. The jokes ricocheted one after another, and though over the passage of time some may be deemed politically incorrect, they

"I never tried to be a phony, never tried to be a star," insisted Diller. "A lot of performers try to be someone else. I never did. I don't know if that's the answer to my longevity in a very competitive business, but it's the only answer I can think of."

"It was the TONight Show that made my career take off, with Jack Paar in New York. It took a lot of shots on that. It takes them a long time to learn your name and if they don't know your name, they won't come back and see you. I finally did make it and it only took me five years to get to Carnegie Hall, which I think is some kind of world record."

—Phyllis Diller

90

were always well-honed and effective. Take, for instance, Diller's story of the hope-lessly homely woman who happened to be covered with rice.

"Did you just get married?" the woman was asked. "No," she replied. "A Chinaman threw up on me."

HERMIONE GINGOLD
HIDDEN JEWEL

Those who recall Hermione Gingold only as the somewhat grotesque Iowa matron in the 1962 movie version of *The Music Man* or as the warbling, over-the-hill courtesan who remembers it well (well, better than Maurice Chevalier did) in the 1958 *Gigi* are missing a good deal of the fun. The tart-tongued, irre-pressible English wit who physically resembled a stuffed owl was truly at her best

Permanently deposited into the pop-culture memory bank for having sat before a painted backdrop as she corrected Maurice Chevalier's faulty memory in the song "I Remember It Well" in 1958's Gigi, *Hermione Gingold possessed a dry humor that was unforgettable in and of itself. Here she is backstage in London, 1959.*

in the days of intelligent American television, especially when the late-night host Jack Paar would let her perch next to him so she could let fly with whatever was on her mind. (Merv Griffin later offered the chair next to his once Paar gave way to Johnny Carson, who preferred Malibu bimbos to bright women of London and New York).* Though sibilant and given to sounding as if she had chewing gum stuck in her throat, Gingold never had problems expressing herself. Asked whether her most recent husband was dead, she took a deep breath and replied, "That's a matter of opinion."

Hermione Ferdinanda Gingold was born in London in 1897, to an English mother and an Austrian father. She began her career in 1911 as a child actor with Noel Coward in *Where the Rainbow Ends,* and gained a following after starring in a series of British revues that proved to be hits with servicemen. "On radio, back in the thirties," recalled BBC personality Barry Took, "she impersonated a character called Mrs. Pullpleasure, who would give a discourse on the joys of playing stringed instruments. Later she played the character of the materfamilias in the radio equivalent of Charles Addams cartoons—*The Dooms.* As Mrs. Doom, served tea by her loyal creature, Trog, a butler of sorts, she was forever at the tea-table, offering her husband the stimulating beverage with a husky, contralto, 'Tea . . . Edmund? Milluk . . . Edmund?,' in a manner that became in its day as renowned as Dame Edith Evans's way of saying, 'A haaandbag?' in *The Importance of Being Earnest."*

Gingold's American stage debut did not come until 1951, in a small revue in Cambridge, Massachusetts. This paved the way for her star-making Broadway vehicle, the 1953 *John Murray Anderson's Almanac,* in which she and the comedian Billy De Wolfe stood out in their skits. "It seems like a long time since anyone acted with as much craft and subtlety," wrote the *New York Times* critic Brooks Atkinson. Yet looking back, subtlety does not seem a word to associate with Gingold. On the eve of her eightieth birthday (she lived to the age of eighty-nine), she remarked that she had always longed to be in *Hedda Gabler* and *Hamlet,* rather than the musicals in which she invariably played. "The trouble with me," she said, "is that I am not considered an actress anymore. I'm a celebrity."

PEARL BAILEY
LOVE OBJECT

As an entertainer, Pearl Bailey would go to practically any extreme to be loved. When in the late sixties she played the matchmaker Dolly Levi in Broadway's *Hello, Dolly!* she trundled down the stage's grand staircase to sing the title song and was greeted with such a roar of approval that she asked the audience, "Want me to come down the stairs again?" And she did.

* Although Carson did use to book Dr. Joyce Brothers.

Primarily a jazz singer, the preacher's daughter from Newport News, Virginia, could never keep from letting an off-the-cuff observation interrupt one of her songs, no matter how serious the moment. After touring with various bands, she made her legitimate debut in Broadway's 1946 *St. Louis Woman*—and got noticed, and notices. "A young lady named Pearl Bailey can sing a song so that it stays sung," judged the *Times,* while the *Journal-American* decided, "Pearl Bailey, who came up from the Village Vanguard to dance and sing in the USO, will be remembered after *St. Louis Woman* is gone." And so she was.

Pearly Mae, as she was called, made a few films, always standing out in what were generally small roles, generally playing a busybody. Where Bailey excelled was in playing herself, a larger-than-life personality whose calling card was the cheer she spread around. President Richard Nixon appointed her the country's

Pearl Bailey used to test strangers she'd meet by holding up her two open palms before them. "What do you see?" she would ask. Amazingly, the lines in one hand perfectly mirrored those in the other. Students of palmistry would say that everything God intended Bailey to achieve (as outlined in her left hand) she did (as shown in her right). And if God didn't say that, then Pearl would.

unofficial Ambassador of Love, one of the few nonpartisan things he ever did. In her later years she devoted much of her time to raising money for AIDS research, and, while not a "funny lady" per se, she managed to entertain and bring a smile to the faces in the crowd, whether they were the audience of a television variety program or in Las Vegas. As she liked to tell people, including interviewers, "Now that we've met, we have a bond. Don't you forget me now."

CAROL BURNETT
VARIETY ARTIST

A Tarzan yell. A tug on her earlobe to send a secret signal home to her grandmother. And perhaps her best television bit ever, when she wore her version of the green velvet gown Scarlett O'Hara fashioned from Tara's parlor curtains—with the curtain rods still in place. "Like my dress?" Carol Burnett asked Rhett Butler (played by her sidekick Harvey Korman). "I saw it in the window and it was just something I couldn't resist."

Thanks to her much-adored, eponymous 1967–79 CBS variety show, for which she collected five Emmys, Burnett (born in 1933) paraded through American living rooms as an entire masquerade-party of characters. The very broad skits in which she was involved carried no contemporary peg, just an old-

What was funny about The Carol Burnett Show *was that the performers were often laughing as hard as the audience. Here at a television-industry banquet, Burnett cozies up to her weekly co-star Harvey Korman, part of her band of merry pranksters (Tim Conway was another). "I was terrified to get up and perform alone," Burnett once admitted. "For me to get up and try to tell a joke, it's sad."*

Left: Once Upon a Mattress, *based upon the fairy tale* The Princess and the Pea, *opened on Broadway in 1959 and helped propel the career of Carol Burnett, here with Joe Bova. But it was television that proved her true forte. That same year she also debuted on* The Garry Moore Show.

Below: *"Once someone in my television audience asked what my measurements were,"* recalled Carol Burnett, here as the cartoonish scrubwoman that became her trademark. *"I said, '37-24-38—but not necessarily in that order.'"*

fashioned ambition to please. Not that Burnett needed to rely on gag writers entirely; she opened her show by fielding ad hoc questions from her in-studio audience, thus displaying her innate gift for the instant comeback. (Those who ever doubted her ability to ad-lib need only see the 1997 documentary *Moon Over Broadway,* which follows Burnett as the headliner in the soulless New York stage farce *Moon Over Buffalo.* One night the set breaks down and Burnett steps before the curtain to keep the house entertained by taking questions. She's not only

quick on her feet, but funny and admirably professional when she had every right to throw a fit.)

Burnett's childhood in San Antonio, Texas, was rough. Her father barely provided for the family. "Think of Jimmy Stewart as an alcoholic," she would say. Mom drank, too, leaving Burnett to be raised in a Hollywood boardinghouse by "Nanny" Mae White, Carol's colorful and loving grandmother who shared her gawky granddaughter's love of the movies. The girl studied theater arts at UCLA, where she and another student so wowed the crowd one night that a benefactor staked them with one thousand dollars to try cracking into the big time in New York. The fellow student was named Don Saroyan. Burnett not only went to New York with him, but married him, in 1954. They went their separate ways a few years later. Burnett's second husband was Joe Hamilton, who produced *The Carol Burnett Show.* They divorced in the eighties.

During that first foray into New York, Burnett broke into television, playing Buddy Hackett's girlfriend Celia on the 1956 live sitcom *Stanley,* in which Buddy Hackett portrayed Stanley Peck, the manager of a newsstand in a New York Hotel (Neil Simon co-wrote the premiere episode). Another role was that of the girl-friend to the Paul Winchell puppet Knucklehead Smiff. Her breakthrough year was 1959: The Off-Broadway musical fairy tale in which she starred, *Once Upon a Mattress,* moved to Broadway, and, after she substituted for Martha Raye one night on the *Garry Moore* television show, she became a regular. From then on the red-head with the ear-to-ear grin was a permanent fixture on the tube. By the century's end, she was a recurring character on the NBC sitcom *Mad About You,* playing the somewhat prickly mother of Helen Hunt's Jamie.

Why the enduring appeal? Bob Mackie, who designed her costumes on her show (including the Scarlett O'Hara curtain-rod number and another outfit with linebacker shoulder-pads for a Joan Crawford spoof called "Mildred Fierce"), liked to refer to his star as "White Bread Woman." "She's so Middle American in her values," he said, "and it's very endearing. She really does laugh like that—because she's the lady next door, who just happens to be funny."

BARBRA STREISAND
THE POWERHOUSE

B arbra Streisand entered the general public's consciousness thanks to her first movie, the 1968 *Funny Girl,* based on her 1964 Broadway vehicle of the same name. It wasn't just a star vehicle. It was a star ballistic missile. Though she'd been a much-discussed fixture on the New York nightclub circuit, opened for "Mr. Show Business" Liberace in Las Vegas, made hit recordings for Columbia Records, and starred in highly visible television specials, the Brooklyn-born dynamo who dressed in secondhand clothing was seldom perceived as little

Streisand as Fanny Brice's Baby Snooks, who appeared only briefly in Funny Girl.

Barbra Steisand's last funny comedy was 1972's What's Up, Doc?, *a mechanical homage to* Bringing Up Baby. *She also acted convincingly as the consummate Jewish liberal in the 1974* The Way We Were. *But she has yet to deliver another tour de force as she did her first time out, in* Funny Girl, *shown here.*

more than a wildly gifted if less-than-photogenic kook with a magical voice. Then came her fantastic screen debut, which delivered to her an Oscar and a mass audience. And though as the years progressed the aggressively Type A–personality star began taking herself so seriously as to thwart any notion of her still being considered a "funny lady," no one would ever sell her short when it came to one commodity: drive.

TOTIE FIELDS
MOTHER MIRTH

While it was said that fat women identified with the size-18 Totie Fields, her audience base was, no pun intended, larger than that. She was born Sophie Feldman and, as a child in Hartford, Connecticut, she pronounced Sophie "Totie," while Fields was an anglicized abbreviation of her real surname. Her aim had been to be a singer and she idolized Sophie Tucker, who once came backstage and advised Totie to take all her money and buy a new wardrobe. The next time Tucker checked in on her young devotee, she declared Totie's appearance "perfect" . . . and Totie knew exactly how to present herself. Among Fields's better gags was her silent impersonation of a fashionable (read bone-thin) saleswoman's reaction to Totie's entrance into the dress department of Bergdorf Goodman. After a slow take in which her eyes widened, Fields's face registered distinct shock, disbelief, and disapproval—as she cricked her elbow to mime the saleswoman's nudging a partner.

Pretending to be a sex object and never posing as a threat to men or women, Totie delivered good-natured, if slightly vulgar routines that generally revolved around her waistline. "Actually," she'd tell audiences, "I'm losing a lot of weight lately." Then, pointing to the cellulite dangling from her arms, she'd add: "See how everything hangs on me?" (Not content to let go of the line after just one laugh, she'd then say in her throaty voice, "Am I right? Am I right?")

Fields was married to the bandleader George Johnston, who managed her career. They had two daughters, Debbie and Jody, and the whole family was fodder for Totie's comedy. No sooner had the girls left home than Totie was raving about how she could again walk naked around the house. Couples, responding to their own suffering with the "empty-nest syndrome," let alone the notion of Totie in the buff, laughed in recognition. Fields went from playing $75-a-week dives in the Northeast to commanding $200,000 a week in the Catskills, Vegas, and Miami Beach, where audiences adored all four-feet-ten-inch-

es of her. She even kept the comedy coming during an entire series of sudden physical tragedies that befell her by the mid-seventies. As a diabetic with circulatory problems, Totie had a facelift that led to complications, including phlebitis, which ultimately led to the amputation of a leg and a dramatic drop in her weight. Undaunted after losing her limb, she presented her new self on Merv Griffin's talk show, where she referred to herself as "Stumpy" as the audience attempted to hold back its collective tears. "At least," the comedienne joked, "I still have a leg to stand on." Woefully, not for long. Totie Fields died August 2, 1978. She was forty-eight.

ELAINE MAY
SMART STUFF

Henrietta Lowell is a bespectacled botanist and a klutz. She is also an heiress. Henry Graham is an effete and fastidious trust-fund baby, except he's an adult—and his money's run out. Of the many comic possibilities to be grabbed by pairing these two diametrically opposed personalities, Elaine May managed to milk nearly all of them in her 1971 film *A New Leaf,* which she wrote, directed, and starred in with Walter Matthau. The movie is but one of May's quietly hysterical accomplishments and is worth focusing on if only because it's so damn funny, as well as touching. Picture the sight of Henrietta with Henry on their honeymoon night (that she is still a virgin goes without question). She's stuck her head through the armhole of her fluffy white nightdress, and Henry can't believe the sight of her. The garment has made Henrietta lopsided. "It's a Grecian-style nightgown," she tells him. "It's very uncomfortable."*

Mike Nichols, May's creative collaborator when the fifties expanded into the sixties, met Elaine May when they were both at the University of Chicago. (He was a student; she was an unregistered drop-in.) While Nichols was appearing in a school stage production, he saw "an evil, hostile girl" who stared at him. That was May. Later in the term he saw her again, this time in a train station waiting room. "May I sit down?" he asked in a crisp, Viennese accent. "Iv you veesh," she replied. A partnership was born.

Elaine (born in Philadelphia in 1932) had learned about show business from her father, the Yiddish actor Jack Berlin. After an early marriage to (and a divorce from) Marvin May, whose name she kept, she studied Method acting. By pairing

Opposite: *In the early nineties, there was just a smidge of Totie Fields to be found in Mike Myers's dead-on impersonation of a verklempte* Jewish mother with her own cable TV talk show in his *"Coffee Talk with Linda Richman" on NBC's* Saturday Night Live. *Coarse, smothering, and well-meaning at the same time—especially when it came to the subject of that "underappreciated" fellow Jewish pearl, Barbra Streisand, who possessed skin "like buttah"—Myers's Richman routine was based on his actual mother-in-law.*

---

* Another good line (of the many): Matthau as Henry is introduced at "the club" to a couple whose name is Hitler. "Are you related to the Boston Hitlers?" he asks. "No," they reply. "We're from Glen Cove."

Ever-sardonic, Mike Nichols and Elaine May (here in their 1960 Broadway Evening) *would constantly revise their routines. One night he was Jack Ego, an insufferable name-dropping TV host, and she was an airheaded Marilyn-like starlet. Another time, they would both drop names, for example:*

NICHOLS: *And then there's Albert Einstein's theory.*

MAY: *Oh, you mean Al. A great dancer. Love his hair.*

NICHOLS: *But, of course, he had to leave Germany because of Adolf Hitler.*

MAY: *Oh, that Dolfie. He was a riot. I used to call him "Cuddles."*

NICHOLS: *Good God!*

MAY: *Oh, Him—a close personal friend of mine.*

up professionally with Nichols shortly after the encounter in the train station, she formed half of what was possibly the sharpest and most successful satirical team in American entertainment history.

Consistently inventive and often improvised, the sketches of Nichols and May involved a gallery of ever-so-slightly exaggerated characters, ranging from a manipulative Jewish mother who sits and waits and waits for her rocket-scientist son to call her (she's sick, she finally confides in him . . . she has to go to the hospital, where "they'll X-ray my nerves"), to an equally manipulative "grief lady" who assists in selling expensive funeral packages (caskets are extra). In one typical example of their drollery, May played a series of AT&T operators who all seemed to have stepped out of a Kafka novel. Nichols was just a poor schnook who wanted to retrieve his last dime so he could make an urgent phone call.

"I watched Elaine," Nichols said in 1998, "and I thought, *She's doing this remarkable thing. She's looking at these people from the outside and the inside at the same time.* It was always real. There was always great forgiveness and sympathy with these people while she was making fun of them. That was her great gift."

Their 1960 Broadway revue *An Evening with Mike Nichols and Elaine May* made them the darling of the cognoscenti, and their routines, recorded on best-selling, long-playing albums, were reproduced live on the television-variety programs of Jack Paar, Steve Allen, Dinah Shore, and Perry Como. The Broadway show ran for more than three hundred performances, though the duo broke up in 1962, after he reportedly smacked her during a routine and she scratched him back and drew blood. While Nichols became a sought-after stage and screen director *(The Graduate, Who's Afraid of Virginia Woolf?,* among others), May began writing and directing, first for the stage, then for the movies. Her scripts were usually far more surefooted than her direction; her 1987 *Ishtar,* starring Warren Beatty and Dustin Hoffman aping the Bing Crosby–Bob Hope *Road* pictures, was a miscalculation on several fronts, though earlier she had wrung a comic gem of a performance out of her daughter, Jeannie Berlin, as the cloying, annoying bride in the laid-back 1972 *The Heartbreak Kid.*

Arguably, Elaine May was at her best writing scripts for Mike Nichols to direct. (They reached a rapprochement in the eighties.) Their 1996 *The Birdcage,* an Americanization of the French cross-dressing farce *La Cage aux Folles,* starred Robin Williams and Nathan Lane and proved an immense popular hit. And while their 1998 adaptation of Joe Klein's thinly disguised savage novel about the Clinton presidential campaign, *Primary Colors,* didn't sell tickets at the box office, May's script for it was among one of the most savvy, entertaining, and effective ever put to paper.

ANNE MEARA
NO SECOND FIDDLE

nitially the comedy team of Jerry Stiller and Anne Meara was considered something of a road-company version of Nichols and May. Such a comparison was not only odious, but also untrue. (Besides their styles being so disparate, all four were friends.) Considered the most realistic husband-and-wife team in stand-up, Stiller and Meara—who were married on September 14, 1954, six days before she turned twenty-four—began doing their domestic routines as Hershey Horowitz and Elizabeth Doyle, often playing up their Brooklyn Jewish/Irish Catholic differences . . . though sometimes what they played up were simply *differences.*

MEARA: I hate you!
STILLER: You hate me? I hate you!
MEARA: You don't know what hate is, the kind of hate I have for you.
STILLER: Listen, my hate for you is such a hot hate, I hate you with heaping hunks of hate!
MEARA: The heat of your hot hate could not begin to approximate the hateful hatredness with which I'm hatefully hating you right now.
STILLER: If it was possible to write the word "Hate" on each grain of sand

in the Sahara Desert, all that hate on each of those hateful grains wouldn't equal one-millionth of the hate that I'm hating you with right now!

MEARA: You know how much you hate me?

STILLER: Yeah.

MEARA: Double it! That's my hate for you!

Their sketches, performed at nightclubs such as New York's Village Vanguard and the Blue Angel, and their evolving success, propelled by guest shots on Ed Sullivan's television program, brought the couple lucrative advertising deals, and they have the distinction of having introduced "a little Blue Nun" to the United States in 1969—on radio advertisements for the wine. (Anne played the fictitious little nun.) Yet their work wasn't tied exclusively to their comic conversational commercials, which they made in abundance, or even to one another. While Jerry may be best remembered for playing George Costanza's father on TV's *Seinfeld,* Anne, it must be noted, scored several acting triumphs, and not only in comedy roles. On stage, she was splendid in John Guare's 1970 production of *The House of Blue Leaves;* on television, she could play anything from the cook on *Archie Bunker's Place* (1979–83) to the gutsy lawyer and title character on *Kate McShane,* the first network dramatic series to feature a woman attorney. And though much of her performance seems to have been left on the cutting room floor, she brought poignancy to her role as the teacher in Alan Parker's 1980 *Fame.* She also proved herself an able dramatist with her Off-Broadway comedy/drama *After-Play.* And while Anne and Jerry's son Ben Stiller, born in 1965, made a real name for himself on TV and in the movies in the nineties—he directed his mother and his sister Amy in his first feature, 1994's *Reality Bites,* before he went on to star in the 1998 gross-out *There's Something About Mary*—if there hadn't been a Stiller and Meara, there certainly would never have been a Ben.

LILY TOMLIN
THINKING WOMAN

Richard Pryor called Lily Tomlin "a goddamn national treasure." Let's just agree and build from there. It's not that the former Mary Jean Tomlin excelled at delivering slam-bang knee-slappers so much as she did at eliciting prolonged smiles and sighs of recognition. Most of the time she made us laugh; a good deal of the time she also made us think.

Tomlin grew up in Detroit, her family having moved there from Kentucky during the Depression (she was born in 1939). In early interviews Tomlin recalled her mother's desire to peek in on Charlotte Ford's debutante party, so Lily bundled Mom—Dad worked as a machinist at the Commonwealth Brass Company—into the car and off they drove to the ritzy, albeit restricted, enclave of Grosse Pointe. Tomlin's distaste for those people who lived on the other side of the brick fence would later surface in her comedy, as she launched subtle broadsides at those whose own restrictions prevented them from understanding the full joys of life.* Tomlin met one such human obstacle early on, her next-door neighbor, Mrs. Rupert. She "wore gloves and fox furs and a hat with a veil to

* Not so Tomlin. When nominated for her supporting performance in Robert Altman's 1975 *Nashville,* in which she played a gospel singer, she showed up at the Oscar ceremony sporting an imitation diamond tiara on her head and a rabbit stole around her shoulders.

TOMLINISMS

* "Why is it when we talk to God we're praying—but when God talks to us, we're schizophrenic?"
* "For fast-acting relief, try slowing down."
* "Reality is the leading cause of stress among those in touch with it."
* "I always wanted to be somebody, but I should have been more specific."
* "If truth is beauty, how come no one has their hair done in the library?"
* "Man invented language to satisfy his deep need to complain."
* "If love is the answer, could you please rephrase the question?"

the day-to-day goings-on in Archie Bunker's household in a lower-middle-class neighborhood of New York. The Goldbergs lived in the Bronx, the Bunkers in Queens, but—and this is a big but—Archie Bunker was no Molly Goldberg. Instead of a wise, nurturing head of the household, Archie (who lived with his wife, his daughter, and his son-in-law) was a right-wing, conservative bigot. Some critics at the time considered him a "lovable bigot," although even then the modifier was questionable. (When the series was rerun on the cable network Nick at Nite in 1998, it carried parental advisories, thanks to Archie's frequent use of such epithets as "hebe," "spade," and "spic"— none of which had aged well; in contrast, when the words were first uttered when the program originated, it was argued that having a buffoon such as Archie say them, in fact, diffused their power.) Archie Bunker, played by Carroll O'Connor, was blue collar, a flag waver, semi-literate, and just downright nasty.

What made the program appealing—and held it together like glue—was Archie's wife, Edith, played by Jean Stapleton. Despite her lack of education and slow brain, Edith had the regal bearing of a Margaret Dumont and the devotion of Lassie. No matter how badly Archie treated Edith, or how outrageous his behavior was toward others, she loved him unequivocally. This wasn't mere comic mugging; this was dramatic acting.

Stapleton, a native New Yorker (born Jeanne Murray, in 1923), was a character actress on stage and in some movies throughout the fifties and sixties before Lear cast her in her defining role. (Contrary to popular belief, she is not related to the actress Maureen Stapleton.) Generally she played the Nervous Nelly neighbor who added further comic relief to musical comedies, roles she pulled off in both the stage and screen versions of *Damn Yankees* and *Bells Are Ringing.* In the Broadway version of *Funny Girl,* she had the distinction of having sung what happens to a wannabe actress "If a Girl Isn't Pretty." She also played drama, many times at the playhouse in Pennsylvania run by her husband, Bill Putch (he died in 1983). Following her departure from *All in the Family* in 1980 she appeared as Mrs. Roosevelt in the 1982 television movie "Eleanor, First Lady of the World." She was also Meg Ryan's wistful colleague in the 1998 Nora Ephron film, *You've Got Mail.*

"The role of Edith was going to bury me if I continued it," said Jean Stapleton, whose Edith Bunker on All in the Family *belongs in the comic pantheon. When she asked to be written out of the show, Stapleton was given a fitting last stand. Despite a life-threatening illness, Edith slaves over a hot stove, preparing corned beef and cabbage for Archie's St. Patrick's Day party. Only after she collapses does her husband learn of her sacrifice. "I ain't nothing without you," he at long last tells her.*

But it is as Archie's adoring "dingbat" that audiences will most likely remember a very gracious lady—one who did not have a high, nasal voice like the one she affected to play Edith. On the other hand, there were some moments of silence that defined Edith, too, such as the time she overheard her daughter, Gloria (Sally Struthers), and son-in-law, Mike Stivic (Rob Reiner), discussing VD. The term confused Edith, until, finally, her frown of concentration faded.

"Oh, now I remember," said Edith. "VD Day."

CHER
CLOTHES HORSE

For a time, it seemed the only entertainment at the annual Oscar ceremony was watching the singer-actress-personality Cher make her entrance in an outrageous headdress and outfit of feathers, spangles, and wire mesh. The appearances sometimes fell under the category of "Laughing at her, not with her." Even worse were her infomercials for hair-care products. Late-night talk host David Letterman and television's satirical *Saturday Night Live* had a field day spoofing her. But Cher has nine lives, if not more. Though at times it seemed she risked becoming the permanent butt of jokes, at the heart of the matter was the fact that hers was the same talent that, self-aware or not, had first entertained America on a kitschy seventies TV show. She then went on to deliver startling dramatic turns in the movies *Silkwood, Mask,* and *Moonstruck,* for which she won the Academy Award as Best Actress. "I can't keep doing the same thing over and over," she once said. "I get bad at it, and I don't want to be bad."

Cherilyn La Piere Sarkisian's mother, Georgia Holt, was married ten times and provided her daughter Cher with an unstable childhood in and around California's San Fernando Valley. As a teen Cher hung out around Hollywood, which is where, in 1963 in a coffee shop frequented by recording-biz types, she met her Svengali, Sonny Bono. She was sixteen; he, twenty-seven. In 1965 they recorded their hippie anthem, "I Got You, Babe," and became stars overnight, segueing into nightclubs (first billed as Caesar and Cleo) and then into television. It was in

Cher with Dick Clark, on TV in 1973, doing a sendup of the 1960s. As the decades progressed, Cher's wild wigs and tattoos gave way to slightly straighter images and some cosmetic surgery. She was a good sport, however, when Today *show hostess Katie Couric introduced her in 1998 by saying Cher was one of the few personalities in show business who was recognizable by one name, "like Charo."*

the latter medium, starting in the summer of 1971, that the Cher look and persona—so beloved of drag queens—took hold. Week after week, wearing one over-the-top Bob Mackie gown after another, Cher would finger her long, flowing brunette hair, stand with her left arm akimbo, and put down the braggadocio Sonny with her wisecracks. His height, his bravado, his male prowess were all sitting targets. Her delivery was playful, yet magisterial.

The Bonos broke up in 1974, and Cher charged Sonny with "involuntary servitude" in the divorce papers. (The next year she married rocker Gregg Allman, and the bumpy union lasted two years.) Yet Cher was there, in January 1998, at Sonny's funeral after a fatal skiing accident. He had, by then, become a California congressman. Combining humorous memories with poignant compliments in her moving eulogy, Cher held back a flood of tears but still managed to insert one of her trademark jibes from the old days. Leave it to Sonny, she said, to have become a Republican.

TREASURED TROIKAS
DREAM TEAMS

The Mary Tyler Moore Show

For seven years in the seventies, Saturday turned into the best night of the week to stay home thanks to a trio of funny ladies: Mary Tyler Moore, Valerie Harper, and Cloris Leachman. On September 19, 1970, they debuted on *The Mary Tyler Moore Show*, starring Moore as Mary Richards, associate news producer at Minneapolis's lowest-rated station, WJM-TV; Harper as Rhoda Morgenstern, her neighbor who worked as a department-store window dresser, and Leachman as their landlady, Phyllis Lindstrom. They were magic together. Mary, hopelessly perky and WASPish; Rhoda, Jewish and neurotic, especially when it concerned her thighs; Phyllis, flighty and bitchy. What made the show compelling and comical was that Mary and her cohorts—including those she worked with at the station*—were more of a family than were any of the supposed nuclear units TV had previously presented. (Were Ozzie and Harriet and their brood ever *really* funny?) Mary was credited with being TV's first believable single career woman—believable for a sitcom, anyway—and she did possess certain characteristics that allowed a huge cross section of the public to identify with her, such as never being able to throw a successful party, and being

* Ed Asner played Mary's gruff boss Lou Grant; Gavin MacLeod was the innocuous news writer Murray Slaughter; Ted Knight was vainglorious and stupid Ted Baxter, the anchorman. When Cloris Leachman left the series to star in her own *Phyllis*, she was replaced by Betty White, as an astringent TV hostess homemaker who predated Martha Stewart, but who also could have served as Martha's prototype.

SUE ANN: Mary, dear—don't the circumstances strike you as being the least bit . . . bizarre?
LOU: After all, the guy died wearing a peanut suit, killed by an elephant.
MURRAY: Yeah—born in a trunk, *died* in a trunk!
MARY: Okay. *Forget* what he was wearing! Suppose he *hadn't* been dressed as a peanut—would it still be funny?
MURRAY: . . . It could have been worse . . . he could have gone as Billy Banana—and had a gorilla peel him to death.

—The Cast of The Mary Tyler Moore Show, from a 1975 Script by David Lloyd, "Chuckles [The Clown] Bites the Dust."

Mary Tyler Moore, the ringmaster who never hogged the spotlight. Real life wasn't always so well balanced. Her overbearing father, a utilities clerk, alienated the young Mary and drove her mother to drink. Mary escaped into "all forms of make-believe," which was show business. Life's harsh realities continued to linger, however. Severest of all was the accidental suicide of Moore's only child, aged twenty-four. Ironically, the tragedy was reminiscent of the 1980 film which brought Moore a Best Actress Academy Award nomination, for Ordinary People.

great-looking, smart, and caring . . . and yet terminally unable to find Mr. Right. Then again, nobody was good enough for Our Mary.

Moore (born 1936, in Brooklyn) entered television in the late fifties as the unseen sexy voice of the secretary Sam on *Richard Diamond, Private Detective,* and became known to audiences as Laurie Petrie on the very urbane *Dick Van Dyke Show,* starting in 1961. Viewers loved her wide grin with its slight overbite, her big brown eyes, her distinctive voice, and the fact she was the first woman in a series to wear a nightgown instead of pajamas. So identifiable was Moore with the Petrie character that when the star and her then-husband, producer Grant Tinker, offered CBS *The Mary Tyler Moore Show,* the network refused to allow Mary's thirtysomething character to be a divorcee for fear of having the audience think she had left Dick Van Dyke.

Harper (born 1940, in Suffern, New York) began as a corps de ballet dancer at New York's Radio City Music Hall before finding her way to Paul Sills's improvisational Story Theater in Chicago. It was there that she found the timing and ease of delivery she needed to nab the role of Rhoda when *The Mary Tyler Moore Show* was being cast. Rhoda seemed so colorful and rife for comic exploitation that she soon spun off into her own sitcom, 1974–78's *Rhoda.* The writing there was never quite up to that on the original show, however, and despite the welcome presence of Nancy Walker (as Rhoda's pushy mother, Ida) and the addition of the talented Julie Kavner (as sister Brenda), *Rhoda* never played as well as *Mary.*

What was so winning about the performances of Cloris Leachman (right) on The Mary Tyler Moore Show *was that the actress never begged to be liked. Hers was undiluted bitchiness, and it worked. Her character, Phyllis, was funny. Likewise Leachman, who once said the secret of growing old gracefully was "never read women's magazines. All that advice will kill you."*

The special one-hour October 28, 1974, wedding of Rhoda Morgenstern (Valerie Harper) to Joe Gerard (David Groh) on Rhoda remains one of American television's highest-rated episodes of all time. Harper followed her most famous sitcom with the 1986–87 series Valerie, which resulted in a nasty lawsuit between her and Lorimar Productions. Lorimar claimed she breached her contract over a financial dispute. Harper insisted she was fired and that Lorimar was trying to ruin her name and reputation. She won. (The jury awarded her $1.8 million plus 12.5 percent of gross profits for the series, which included money for episodes in which she did not appear.) In 1998, ABC promised a reunion series with Mary Tyler Moore and Valerie Harper as Mary and Rhoda, but the project was shelved pending a search for better scripts, the network said. Harper chose to bide her time by starring in a one-woman stage show as the author-humanitarian Pearl Buck.

112

Raspy-voiced Julie Kavner (born in 1950) got her start playing the younger sister, Brenda Morgenstern, on Rhoda, and throughout her career has specialized in playing, as she admitted, "a nice person." That included being the voice behind Marge Simpson (and Marge's two sisters, Patty and Selma) on The Simpsons, as well as appearing in numerous Woody Allen movies—in which she has played both his mother (in Radio Days) and his girlfriend (in New York Stories). Amazingly, for so New York a "type," Kavner has never lived in the East, being a total product of Southern California, though her parents, David and Rose Kavner, originally were from the Bronx. As Kavner told an interviewer when she starred in This Is My Life, Nora Ephron's 1992 comedy about a single mother who dreams of being a stand-up comic, she never considered herself the least bit amusing. "When I was a kid I would get upset when people laughed at me when I didn't mean to be funny. I would always hear: 'We're not laughing at you. We're laughing with you.' But I would say, 'I'm not laughing.'"

"There was a funny little kid who used to hang around backstage at the Winter Garden when her pop [the acrobat Dewey Barto] had his act in the Olsen and Johnson shows [Hellzappopin' (1938)] and daytimes she would answer the casting calls. Any casting calls. She wasn't particular. George Abbott had a casting call for Best Foot Forward *[1941] and she answered that one. She sluffed across the stage, did a double take at the work light, and Abbott fell out of his chair."* So wrote Robert Sylvester, the theater critic for New York's Daily News, January 30, 1948. Nancy Walker (born in Philadelphia as Anna Myrtle Swoyer in 1922) became known for playing brassy, loud-mouthed cut-ups. (Shown here in 1958, Walker is dolled up for a New York charity ball.) On The Mary Tyler Moore Show *she played Ida Morgenstern, Rhoda's indomitable mother, and her role expanded when Rhoda got a series of her own. Besides Ida, Walker played* McMillan and Wife's *scrappy housekeeper on Rock Hudson's and Susan St. James's 1971–76 television series, and throughout the seventies she pushed paper towels as a diner waitress in commercials for Bounty, "the quicker picker-upper." She died in 1992.*

Leachman (born 1926, in Des Moines) did local radio as a teen prior to studying drama at Northwestern. In 1946 she was crowned Miss Chicago, then became a Miss America runner-up. The honor brought her to New York, where she began acting on the stage and in live TV dramas as early as 1948, on the *Kraft Television Theatre* and *Philco Television Playhouse.* She played the mother on the *Lassie* series from 1957 to 1958, and the very same year she appeared in *Mary Tyler Moore,* she was nominated for a Best Supporting Actress Academy Award, for Peter Bogdanovich's adaptation of the Larry McMurtry novel *The Last Picture Show.* Far from playing for laughs, Leachman portrayed a neglected wife who entered into an adulterous affair with a much younger man. As quick-tongued off-screen as she was on, Leachman complained that her love interest in the movie, the actor Timothy Bottoms, didn't bathe, which is really why she deserved the Oscar.

Concurrent with her double-Emmy-winning run on *Mary Tyler Moore*—which was followed by her 1975–77 spin-off *Phyllis*—Leachman was put to hilarious use by Mel Brooks in his *Young Frankenstein* and *High Anxiety* (1974 and 1978, respectively). In the former, she played the notorious Frau Blucher, whose very name caused horses to shriek; in the latter, she was Nurse Diesel, a rather masculine attendant at a sanitarium—if her pencil-line mustache under her nose was any indication. In 1993 she was permitted to chew up the scenery again, stepping into the Irene Ryan TV role of Granny Clampett in the movie version of *The Beverly Hillbillies.* She was her funny old self; the movie wasn't.

How enduring is *The Mary Tyler Moore Show*? Very, and not merely in reruns or as an inspiration to *Ally McBeal.* In the mid-nineties, Joan Jett recorded a version of the sitcom's theme song, "Love Is All Around," reinterpreting it as a chick-rock anthem for its time.

The Golden Girls

Little old ladies were from Pasadena. And they were supposed to be sweet. And act old. At least that's what radio, television, and the movies had dictated. Furthermore, old was forty, especially for a woman. That's what the jokes said. So enter NBC's *The Golden Girls,* presented by *Soap*-creator Susan Harris, said to be the first series in television history in which all the stars were female—and over *fifty.* And their characters were all libidinous. As a result of that and the chemistry between the actresses, the show, which debuted in 1985 (it ran for seven seasons), finished in the Nielsen ratings' Top Ten in each of its first five seasons. Broadway veteran Beatrice Arthur, who had already starred in her own hit 1972–78 series *Maude* (an *All in the Family* spin-off, wherein Maude was introduced as Archie Bunker's liberal cousin), played the retired teacher Dorothy Zbornak, a divorcee. Betty White, who seemed to have been on television since the beginning of the medium (but who had scored as the hypersexed "Happy

Before The Golden Girls *there was the 1954–59* December Bride, *starring veteran character actress* **Spring Byington** *(1893–1971) as Lily Ruskin, a widow who lived with her daughter and son-in-law, and* **Verna Felton** *(1890–1966) as Hilda Crocker, Lily's comic comrade in arms. The two older women did date, though not as ferociously as would the Golden Girls; Hilda's boyfriend was Stanley, an insect exterminator. Byington, a Colorado native who made her stage debut in a Denver stock company at the age of fourteen, made more than a hundred movies over her career, usually playing a well-meaning neighbor (as she did in* Dodsworth, *1936) or a daffy mother (*You Can't Take It With You, *1938, which brought her an Oscar nomination). Felton had an extensive radio career, often playing a battle-ax mother-in-law, though Disney fans will recognize her voice as that of the busybody elephant in* Dumbo *and the fairy godmother in* Cinderella—*the one who sings "Bibbity Bobbity Boo." (The character with them in the photo is character actor Will Wright.)*

Possibly the funniest lady "of a certain age" on television was **Marion Lorne** *(1886–1966), who elevated stuttering to an art. Whether playing the landlady Mrs. Gurney on the Wally Cox sitcom about the milquetoast schoolteacher Mr.* Peepers *(1952–55), or Samantha's dotty Aunt Clara opposite Elizabeth Montgomery on* Bewitched *(1964–68), Lorne was a dithery delight. The character actress was born in Wilkes Barre, Pennsylvania, and enjoyed an extensive stage career in England. Garry Moore cast her as a regular on his variety show, and she was so popular with small-screen audiences that she starred in a 1958 television production of* Harvey, *about the invisible rabbit. Sadly, Lorne—who was said to be equally befuddled in person—died before the release of Mike Nichols's 1967* The Graduate, *in which she played the confused member of the wedding party who greets the uninvited Benjamin Braddock in the hotel lobby, just as he's arranging his first dangerous liaison with Mrs. Robinson.*

Homemaker" Sue Ann Nivens on *The Mary Tyler Moore Show),* was the dippy grief counselor Rose Nylund. Rue McClanahan played the steel magnolia museum worker Blanche Devereaux. Estelle Getty, who played Harvey Fierstein's nagging mother in Broadway's *Torch Song Trilogy,* was Sophia Petrillo, the still-cranky and free-speaking mother of Dorothy who moved into the Miami condo shared by the other three women when her retirement home burned down. Though the women's philosophy was "best friends forever," they still managed to dis each other. Typical was this exchange, when Blanche (McClanahan) asked, "Rose, what was your first impression of me?" Answered her pal (Betty White) with a smile: "I thought you wore too much makeup and were a slut." Pause. "I was wrong. You don't wear too much makeup."

The Golden Girls pretty much lived on two sets: their salmon-and-wicker living room, and their kitchen, home to their late-night cheesecake–eating binges. From left, the Girls are Estelle Getty, Beatrice Arthur, Rue McClanahan, and Betty White in 1990.

The First Wives Club

An inspired stroke of casting brought together Bette Midler, Goldie Hawn, and Diane Keaton for the 1996 comedy *The First Wives Club,* very loosely based on Olivia Goldsmith's novel about three divorced women who seek revenge on their exes. Paul Rudnick peppered Robert Harlin's script with deft one-

Three characters in search of revenge. From left, Goldie Hawn, Diane Keaton, and Bette Midler in The First Wives Club (1996).

liners, though the entire theme of the picture could be summed up by the philosophy espoused on-screen by the noted real-life ex-spouse Ivana Trump: "Don't get mad. Get everything." Better yet, get a load of the stars.

BETTE MIDLER

Bette Midler was once described by Mark Rydell, who directed her first movie, 1979's *The Rose*, as "a nice little Jewish girl from Honolulu—with a nuclear power plant in her stomach." That will do. Naughty, bawdy, campy, vampy, and capable of standing alone at Radio City Music Hall and filling the entire stage with her presence, Midler could from one moment to the next both satirize and sentimentalize a wide variety of cultural references, most of which—such as the song "Boogie Woogie Bugle Boy"—you otherwise might have thought you wanted to leave behind.

Bette won her first talent contest when she was in the sixth grade. She sang "Lullaby of Broadway" and copped the two-dollar grand prize. Her father was a transplanted house painter from New Jersey who worked for the navy, and theirs was the only Jewish family in a primarily Samoan neighborhood. In the summer, from the ages of thirteen to fifteen, Bette—named for her mother's favorite film star, Bette Davis—would work at the Dole pineapple processing factory, "removing the bad ends" from the fruit.

By the time she was twenty-one, in 1966, she was in her first movie, *Hawaii*—as an extra. Moving to New York after dropping out of the University of

Bette Midler once admitted that she used a postage scale to determine how heavy her breasts were. "I won't tell you how much they weigh," she announced to her appreciative concert audience, "but it cost $87.50 to ship them to Brazil. Third class."

Oscar. Her biggest screen hit was 1980's *Private Benjamin,* a simple concept—a Jewish-American Princess finds herself in the army—played out beautifully. She not only became a full-fledged movie star but a Hollywood producer with clout. With rare exception, though, most of her movies afterward were limp *Benjamin* clones, until *First Wives Club.* In it, she poked fun at herself by parodying a vain, collagen-enhanced Hollywood actress who's played too cute too long.

And yet, cute she was. In 1996, she danced a surreal Astaire-Rogers number along the banks of the Seine with Woody Allen in his offbeat musical *Everyone Says I Love You.* Since 1983 she has lived with the actor Kurt Russell. "I'm smarter than people give me credit for," says Hollywood's favorite dumb blond. "I have a lite-personality and a deep-thinking brain."

DIANE KEATON

Woody Allen once said that the funniest person he knew was his wife from 1966 to 1970, Louise Lasser—and better known to the public as the star of the 1976 soap-opera parody *Mary Hartman, Mary Hartman.* Yet Woody's greatest muse had to be Diane Keaton, his romantic partner and co-star during the seventies. Under her floppy hats, baggy clothes, and constant air of befuddled exasperation—signaled by her cry of, "Oh, lah-de-dah"—Keaton became a movie icon and an Oscar winner thanks to Allen's 1977 *Annie Hall,* before segueing away from Allen and Annie-like roles toward becoming a more fully rounded artist, photographer, and director herself.

Her real name, in fact, was Diane Hall, born (in 1946) and raised in sleepy Santa Ana, California, in conservative Orange County. (Keaton was her mother's maiden name.) At nineteen Diane was an understudy Off-Broadway in the counter-culture musical *Hair,* and within two years she was starring opposite Woody in his 1969 play *Play It Again, Sam,* which was filmed with Allen and Keaton in 1972. By then Keaton's star was well on the rise—witness her role in *The Godfather,* also 1972, as Al Pacino's girlfriend and then wife—though her style was not to everyone's taste. "Her work, if that is the word for it, always consists chiefly of dithering, blithering, neurotic coming apart at the seams—an acting style that is really a nervous breakdown in slow-motion," complained the critic John Simon.

She continued to delight Woody, however. Besides *Annie Hall,* he had used her in his 1973 *Sleeper,* then his more serious *Love and Death* (1975), and later in *Manhattan* (1979), *Radio Days* (1987), and his underrated *Manhattan Murder Mystery* (1993). She was amusing, too, in the (non-Woody) very slick 1987 *Baby Boom,* about a yuppified New York career woman suddenly handed a toddler to raise, and opposite Steve Martin in a remake of the old wedding-jitters warhorse *Father of the Bride* (1991).

Often less successful were her dramas. Warren Beatty's 1981 $43-million *Reds,* a David Lean–like epic about American journalist John Reed, with Keaton as

the free thinker Louise Bryant, bled red at the box office, as did the 1983 adaptation of novelist John Le Carré's *The Little Drummer Girl,* with Keaton in the lead.

MADELINE KAHN THE CHAMELEON

In Peter Bogdanovich's 1972 *What's Up, Doc?,* while Barbra Streisand and Ryan O'Neal were trying like crazy to ape the behavior of Katharine Hepburn and Cary Grant in *Bringing Up Baby,* newcomer Madeline Kahn stepped forward as O'Neal's shrill, ball-breaking fiancée Eunice and damn near stole the picture. Bogdanovich used her again as the sashaying slut in *Paper Moon,* an affectionate tribute to Depression-era whimsy, but it was Mel Brooks who truly displayed Kahn

New York was seldom more romantic or funny than when Diane Keaton and Woody Allen collaborated on Annie Hall. *Both had come of age as artists—he as an actor-writer-director and she as a leading lady. The movie won the Best Picture Oscar, and she was named Best Actress.*

to her best advantage. Parodying Marlene Dietrich's Lili Marlene as Lily Von Schtup ("I'm Tired") in Brooks's 1974 western send-up *Blazing Saddles* and then as Elsa Lanchester's classic monster-bride in his *Young Frankenstein* (also 1974), Kahn seemed to be having just as much a good time as her audiences.

Born in Boston but reared in New York, Kahn made her professional debut at the age of six, in 1948, on radio's *Horn and Hardart's Children's Hour.* "I cried on the air," she remembered, "and they dragged me off the second time I was on." Possessed of an operatic soprano, she did Musetta in *La Bohème* in Washington before joining Juilius Monk's *Upstairs at the Downstairs* comedy cabaret in 1966. It was her comic performance in the film short *The Dove,* which satirized Ingmar Bergman movies, that got her the attention of Bogdanovich, which in turn got her the attention of Brooks.

Kahn's heyday was clearly the seventies, though she never lost her talent to amuse. In 1978 she took the Carole Lombard role in a Broadway musical version of *Twentieth Century,* but dropped out of the production mid-run for reasons never clearly explained. For television she tried her hand at two series: *Oh Madeline,* from 1983 to 1984, and *Mr. President,* in 1989, which proved a busy year for her. That spring she co-starred with Ed Asner in a Broadway revival of *Born Yesterday;* though the production lacked sparkle, it did lead to Kahn's landing the role of

Two accomplished mimics: Gilda Radner (left) greeted Madeline Kahn at the 1984 wedding reception of Gilda and Gene Wilder. On one memorable episode of Saturday Night Live, Gilda did her Barbara Wawa (Walters) as if the newswoman were interviewing Madeline's Marlene Dietrich. There wasn't a letter "r" to be heard.

The actress who served as the role model for Kahn's horny bride in *Young Frankenstein* was herself a great eccentric, the English-born **Elsa Lanchester** (1902–1986). It was she who donned the Brillo-and-lightning-streaked wig and hissed like a cat in director James Whale's eerily effective *The Bride of Frankenstein* (1935).

Lanchester—pronounced *Lancaster*—began acting when she was sixteen, after having danced as a child with Isadora Duncan's troupe in Paris. In 1929 she married the great actor Charles Laughton, and in 1934 they appeared together in *The Private Life of Henry VIII,* she as Anne of Cleves. The next year they emigrated to Hollywood. In *Bell, Book, and Candle,* the 1958 version of the John Van Druten play, she played a ditzy medium, and in 1964's *Mary Poppins* she breezed in and out of the Banks household as the nanny who couldn't handle the children. She even had a go with Lucy Ricardo on an episode in which Lucy and Ethel drove to Florida. They were convinced Lanchester was an ax murderer. As she told interviewer James Watters in the early eighties, "I guess everyone has to grow old in their own way, but I hope I keep a sense of humor until the end."

What made Madeline Kahn so consistently funny was that she seldom removed her tongue from her cheek. Here she is in Mel Brooks's Young Frankenstein *before her transformation into the monster's oversexed bride.*

"Gorgeous" in Wendy Wasserstein's 1992 comedy-drama *The Sister's Rosensweig.* She played the happy-on-the-outside, crying-on-the-inside sister who wore faux Chanel in order to make her failing husband look more successful. Kahn won a Tony for it.

JOAN RIVERS
THE MOUTH

Understatements need not apply here. Joan Rivers is the person who said that women in France are so ugly that Willie Nelson came in Number Two in the Miss France contest. When Jacqueline Kennedy married Aristotle Onassis, Rivers said, "I respect Jackie Onassis! Marrying that old fat ass! A few schtups and *bang!* You walk away with twenty-six [million] big ones!" The Royal Family: "A bunch of dogs! Go out on the street, call their names—Queenie, Duke, Prince. See what shows up!" The Queen herself: "Is that a schlep? If you own England, Ireland, Scotland, and Canada—shave your legs!" To a woman in her nightclub audience who has just become engaged: "If he wants the ring back, you swallow the stone. No man will look through shit for a diamond." As for herself: "I was the ugliest child ever born in Larchmont, New York. Oh, please! The doctor looked at me and slapped my mother."

One of the most desperate and successful women ever to swim the treacherous waters of stand-up, Rivers flowed from Barnard College, where she graduated Phi Beta Kappa, to Seventh Avenue, where she toiled in the rag trade as a fashion coordinator for a clothing firm. (She even married the boss's son, though the union lasted but six months.) Comedy beckoned, however, and her fierce desire to make it big even caused her and her second husband and manager Edgar Rosenberg to mortgage their home when she wrote and directed her first film, 1978's *Rabbit Test.* But it was Johnny Carson who proved both a blessing and a bane to the Rivers career: in 1966 he gave her her first national exposure on his show. By 1983 she was named permanent guest host whenever Johnny took a day off, which was many a day. Her monologues—particularly those concerning Elizabeth Taylor's girth—were wildly hilarious, and about as tasteless as one could be on television. People tuned in simply to see how outrageous she would be. But when Joan learned that she wasn't in the running to replace Carson when he retired, she accepted a $3 million offer and a three-year contract from Rupert Murdoch's fledgling Fox network to host her own late-night program. When she called Johnny to tell him the news (which he'd already heard), he wouldn't so much as take her call. "I'm the only woman in the history of the world who left Johnny Carson and didn't ask him for money," Rivers said of her much-married former friend.

JOAN RIVERS ON ELIZABETH TAYLOR

* "Her thighs have gone condo."
* "She has more chins than the Hong Kong phone book."
* "She pressed her ears and they bled gravy."
* "She puts mayonnaise on aspirin."
* "Mosquitoes see her and scream, 'Buffet!'"
* "Her car has a bumper sticker that says, 'My other car is a refrigerator'"

And Elizabeth Taylor's reaction? "Honey," the star told Rivers, "those jokes don't get me where I live."

The Fox show did not succeed. Its failure and his being depressed from a heart attack he had recently suffered were cited as the reasons Edgar Rosenberg killed himself in 1987. After their twenty-two years together, Joan's life went into a tailspin. She became bulimic. ("Bulimia was wonderful. It ruins your insides, it ruins your teeth, and it stops your heartbeat. But—how great it was to have all I wanted to eat and throw it up.") She could not find work; her agent told her, "Nobody wants to see a woman whose husband has just committed suicide." And she and their daughter Melissa stopped speaking, although they eventually patched things up, and Joan's career was revived. Mother and daughter starred in "Tears and Laughter: The Joan and Melissa Rivers Story," a network made-for-TV movie about this chapter of their lives (they played themselves), then they took to appearing

together on an "E!" entertainment cable-network program, rubbing shoulders with stars and then gossiping about them behind their backs.

DOROTHY LOUDON
SHOWSTOPPER

Until her 1977 Tony-winning triumph in the Broadway musical *Annie*—in which she played the hilariously mean-spirited orphanage matron Miss Hannigan—Dorothy Loudon had given so many stellar performances in so many disappointing shows that she had earned the nickname "Queen of the Flops." "What is good?" the *New York Times* critic Clive Barnes wrote of the 1969 musical by Alan Sherman,* *Fig Leaves Are Falling.* "One tremendous thing called Dorothy Loudon. She stopped the show—at least would have stopped it had it ever been properly started. Loudon is lovely, adorable, beautiful, wonderful, superb, and the kind of girl every man wants to call mother. She has a voice from way back when, and a gleam in her eye never fiercer than when facing deflation. The important thing about her is that she is both lovable and vulnerable, so much so that I feel personally affronted at the way this show wastes her."

* Best known for the child's letter-from-camp song, "Hello, Muddah, Hello Faddah."

New Englander Dorothy Loudon, here in an early television appearance, is one of the great treasures of American musical comedy. At a tribute to Stephen Sondheim, she raised the roof with her medley of his "Losing My Mind" and "You Could Drive a Person Crazy"—by pretending to lose her mind as she was singing. Said Sondheim to her afterward: "You don't know how good you are."

There were a few more flops between *Fig Leaves* and *Annie,* but there also had been supper-club and lounge-act successes (her venues—Ruban Blue, the Blue Angel, Mister Kelly's—were the cream of the class), to say nothing of striking appearances on television variety shows, most notably Garry Moore's, where she first appeared in late 1962, after Carol Burnett had left. But while Burnett made her name on TV, Loudon made hers with live audiences. She studied at the American Academy of Dramatic Arts and spent summers at Pennsylvania's Camp Tamiment resort, a proving ground run by *Your Show of Shows* producer Max Liebman whose alumnae included Sid Caesar, Imogene Coca, Jerome Robbins, and Danny Kaye. Loudon, who shared her dressing room there with Elaine May, also met and performed at Tamiment with the young songwriter Fred Ebb and the young comedy writer Woody Allen. Yet despite the formal training, Loudon relied primarily on instinct when she took to the stage, to the point that she seemed to possess ESP when it came to reading audiences. "I reach back and get it from somewhere," she once explained to *New York Times* interviewer Judy Klemesrud. "I don't know where. . . . Something's working up in my head."

Some higher power was also toiling in her corner the afternoon Mike Nichols, who was producing *Annie,* ran into her in a Manhattan rehearsal hall and offered her the role of Hannigan. "At first I didn't want it," recalled Dorothy. "There's an old saying, 'Never be in a show with kids, dogs, or an Irish tenor,' and this show had all three." It also ended up containing some classic Loudon ad libs, which managed to find their way into the musical's book. Among them: "Why a kid would want to be an orphan, I'll never know."

Loudon stopped the show with her 1977 Tony-acceptance speech when she compared the sequined gown she was wearing to the shimmering curtain behind her ("I always knew I could play this room," she declared), and the Tony show producer Alexander H. Cohen relied on her as a presenter for the next several years—rarely bothering to fashion a script for her. Loudon went on to co-star with Katharine Hepburn in 1981, in the Ernest Thompson play *West Side Waltz,* and Hepburn said of Dorothy: "We haven't even begun to see what she can really do. And not just comedy." In Chicago, Loudon won the Sarah Siddons Award for her acting in *Waltz,* and triumphed in that city again when she played the lead in *Driving Miss Daisy* there. Yet Dorothy also proved a successful laugh-getter and, not surprisingly, an adept farceur when the knockabout British comedy *Noises Off* came to Broadway in 1983. (Coincidentally, when both *Annie* and *Noises Off* were turned into movies, Carol Burnett played the Loudon roles. The chemistry was never quite the same.)

By the nineties, the onetime "Queen of Flops" was now "Queen of Benefits" at charity concerts, saying "There's not a disease I haven't played for." She played again in September of 1998, when she appeared with Julie Andrews and other Broadway divas in the Carnegie Hall concert for the Public Broadcasting System's "Great Performances" series, *My Favorite Broadway—The Leading Ladies.* Loudon sang her eleven o'clock number "Fifty Percent" from *Ballroom,* the 1978 Michael Bennett musical in which she had starred. And she stopped the show.

GILDA RADNER
HAPPY FACE

When *Saturday Night Live* premiered on NBC at eleven-thirty P.M. on October 11, 1975, it introduced a hipper version of what Sid Caesar was doing on Saturday nights in the forties and fifties, but the debt to Caesar was evident. And while *SNL* lacked a Caesar-esque leading man—though Chevy Chase would have been the obvious candidate

Gilda as Emily Litella, fierce and upright, yet wrong-headed and quick to surrender. She couldn't understand what all the fuss was about saving "Soviet jewelry." Never mind.

had he stayed on the show beyond its first season—the program did have its own Imogene Coca: Gilda Radner. There wasn't anything she couldn't do. Furthermore, there was nothing she wouldn't do, including discussing nose "boogers" as one of her characters, the abrasive, gum-chewing newscaster Roseanne Rosannadanna, an editorialist who ended every footloose commentary by saying, "It's always something!"

Ah, Gilda. One critic in 1979 appropriately described her as a "thirty-three-year-old woman who appears to have a Band-Aid on her knee." She came from an upper-middle-class Jewish family in Detroit—her mother named her after the sultry Rita Hayworth movie character, her wealthy father died when she was fourteen—and she majored in education at the University of Michigan. She started in comedy after heading (with her then-boyfriend) to Toronto, where she joined the Canadian branch of Chicago's Second City improvisational group.* With another Second City member, John Belushi, she starred in "The National Lampoon Radio Hour" and the live "National Lampoon Show," in 1974. The following year, she was the first person signed for *SNL.* Producer Lorne Michaels was so impressed with Gilda that he did not even bother to audition her.

Roseanne Rosannadanna, another Gilda alter ego, fashioned after a New York newscaster, Roseanne Scamardella, who was said to have found backhanded homage amusing. Gilda's Roseanne, however, had problems with personal hygiene that she liked to announce on the air, such as having a booger stuck in her nose. Television audiences had never heard that type of thing before.

She sparkled on *SNL,* and was the one star on the show who would giggle at the antics of her fellow performers, as she did during the skit in which Dan Aykroyd was playing a repairman who kept exposing his butt crack. Her own cast of characters included the nerdy Lisa Loopner, six-year-old Judy Miller, high-haired interviewer Barbara Wawa (as in Walters, who had a speech impediment), and the

do-gooder little old lady Emily Litella, who seldom got her words right. "What's this I hear about making Puerto Rico a steak?" Emily demanded to know. "The next thing they'll be wanting is a salad, and then a baked potato!" When made aware of her malapropism, Emily would say a defeated, "Never mind."

When she left the *SNL* in 1980, Gilda went on to star in a one-woman Broadway show, *Gilda Live!,* which was filmed the following year by director Mike Nichols. It turned out to be her best film, though she did make a series of comedies with her second husband, Gene Wilder. (Her first husband, during a brief marriage, had been a musician on *SNL,* G. E. Smith, and she and Bill Murray had had a romance.)

During the making of 1985's *Haunted Honeymoon* she started to feel stomach cramps, and was diagnosed, in October of 1986, with ovarian

* Among the women graduates of the two Second City troupes: Mary Gross, Valerie Harper, Barbara Harris, Madeline Kahn, Shelley Long, Andrea Martin, Elaine May, Anne Meara, Catherine O'Hara, Mary Steenburgen, and Betty Thomas.

cancer. She took to writing a book about her struggle (eventually published posthumously, titled *It's Always Something)* and managed to make some guest appearances on television. But the cancer was ferocious. On a Saturday morning in May 1989, Gilda died. That night on *Saturday Night Live,* Steve Martin introduced a clip from a previous show in which he and Gilda had burlesqued Fred Astaire and Cyd Charisse's *pas de deux* from the movie *The Bandwagon,* in which their passion for their dance made them overlook the fact they were bumping into one another and destroying the studio. It was delightful and funny. And that was Gilda.

WHOOPI GOLDBERG SURPRISE!

I f anyone had dared to predict in 1984, when she premiered in her own critical-
ly acclaimed one-woman Broadway show, that fourteen years later Whoopi
Goldberg would be starring as the center square in a revival of television's *The
Hollywood Squares,* he would have been shot as a subversive. But go know. The
Whoop-ster had been in worse vehicles (practically any of her movies between
1986's *Jumpin' Jack Flash* and 1990's *Ghost)* and still came up smelling like a
rose. Her star started rising in 1983, after Mike Nichols caught her act—called
Spook Show—in Berkeley and moved her to Broadway for a one-woman show.
Among the characters she pulled out of the trunk in her head: Fontaine, an
uptown junkie who ends up crying in Anne Frank's secret room in Amsterdam. Her
material, which attacked hypocrisy and suppression, bordered on the angry, but
she was fresh and startling, and who couldn't be amused simply by her name?
(She had wanted to call herself Whoopi Cushion—she was born Caryn Johnson,
in 1949, in a Manhattan housing project—but her mother warned her that
people might not take her seriously.) She was compared to Elaine May, Lily
Tomlin, and Groucho Marx, though Moms Mabley and Lenny Bruce seemed
to fit into the formula, too. With all that, and her trademark dreadlocks, she
was still original. Steven Spielberg cast her in *The Color Purple,* but not
until *Ghost*—as a jive-talking medium—did she catch on in movies. She
won the Best Supporting Actress Oscar for that, and then scored on
her own as a Reno lounge singer disguised as a nun in 1991's
Sister Act. Bouncing from TV (a *Star Trek* spin-off), to the stage
(taking over for Nathan Lane in a revival of *A Funny Thing
Happened on the Way to the Forum,* and co-hosting with Billy
Crystal and Robin Williams the annual *Comedy Relief* benefit for the
homeless), to the occasional movie, Goldberg—an old family name, she

*Whoopi Goldberg, here at a 1990
benefit as a dreamy, blue-eyed
blond, never shied away from con-
troversy. At the time she was dating the actor Ted Danson, she
was roasted by the Friars Club.
He showed up in blackface.
Members were outraged.
Whoopi wanted to know
what all the fuss
was about.*

" A nd, like, just as I was going out the door I passed this big dude
walking 'round in circles with a picket sign, talkin' 'bout 'Stop
Abortion.' So I said, 'Motherfucker, when was the last time you
was pregnant?' And he looks at me, he says, 'I don't have to discuss
that with you.' I said, 'Oh, but you should, because I have the answer
to abortion.' He said, 'What is it?' I said, 'Shoot your dick."

—Whoopi Goldberg, as Fontaine, a Harlem drug dealer

said—is said to be reaping $7 million a year from her stint as the center Hollywood Square. Someone's laughing all the way to the bank.

TRACEY ULLMAN
SPLIT PERSONALITIES

Tracey Ullman never really had high ratings on U.S. television, but she sure had charisma—and critical approbation. Something of a high-strung British cross between Carol Burnett and Robin Williams, Ullman herself admitted that there's one thing she can always guarantee to be, "irritating." Americans first got a load of her when she co-starred with Meryl Streep in the 1985 movie *Plenty*, set in England during World War II. By then Ullman, who was born in 1959 and educated at the Italia Conti Stage School, had already cut an album parodying Connie

When Mike Nichols first presented Whoopi on Broadway in 1983, he called her "one part Elaine May, one part Groucho, one part Ruth Draper, one part Richard Pryor, and five parts never-before-seen." Here she is in 1992's Sister Act. *A one-time bricklayer and mortuary cosmetologist, Goldberg once admitted, "The greatest thing I was ever able to do was give a welfare check back. I brought it back to the welfare department and said, 'Here, I don't need this anymore.'"*

Francis's bubble-gum music of the fifties, *You Broke My Heart in Seventeen Places.* Ullman had appeared on her side of the Atlantic in an eighties' British-style version of *Saturday Night Live* called *Three of a Kind,* and then took a break in 1986 to have a child, Mabel, after marrying the millionaire TV producer Allen McKeown. Her Fox television program *The Tracey Ullman Show,* produced by *The Mary Tyler Moore Show* veteran James L. Brooks and choreographed by Paula Abdul, debuted in the spring of 1987 and took that year's Best Comedy Series Emmy away from such worthy competitors as David Letterman and *SNL.* On the *Tracey* show she played a wide variety of recurring roles of both sexes, including Kay, the tiresome secretary; Tina, a New York postal employee; and Francesca, a teen being raised by her gay father and his lover. (Among its other distinctions, the show introduced *The Simpsons,* which began as an animated short.) Once the show ceased production in 1990, Ullman tried the stage and screen, but was back where she seemingly belonged, on the small screen, when HBO signed her for a series of specials. "I love California!," the transplanted Tracey declared of her new home. "Who wouldn't? There are so many Brits here."

RENEE TAYLOR
SECRET WEAPON

The *Nanny* debuted on CBS in 1993 and made a star out of its Queens (New York) princess, Fran Drescher, who played Fran Fine. The following year, the sitcom added another character, that of Fran's mother, Sylvia, played by Renee Taylor. Now *there's* a funny woman. The same year she played Eva Braun in Mel Brooks's "Springtime for Hitler" in his musical play within his 1968 movie *The Producers.* Taylor and her husband, Joe Bologna, wrote and starred in the Broadway comedy *Lovers and Other Strangers,* which they then adapted for a 1970 screen version. Since then their work together has been consistently funny and connected to the male-female aspects of life, especially the arguments. No sooner has he frequently said, "That's it! I'll never work with you again," then the moment manages to find its way into the scene they're writing.

Renee Wexler was born in the thirties and grew up in the Bronx. Graduating from the Academy of Dramatic Arts, she started acting with improv groups in the fifties and became a frequent guest on Jack Paar's talk show before she drifted into comedy writing. She and Bologna married in 1965 (it was her second marriage), and the wedding reception was held on *The Merv Griffin Show.*

The Bolognas divide their time between homes in New Jersey and Beverly Hills, because, as she told David Letterman, "One keeps us real, the other keeps us phony." Their last play together was 1996's *Bermuda Avenue Triangle,* about a ménage à trois in a Florida retirement community. (Beatrice Arthur played the third member of the party in the Los Angeles production, Nanette Fabray in New York.)

Renee Taylor with Fran Drescher, in her familiar role as the mother on television's The Nanny. *But in 1968, Taylor was Eva Braun to Dick Shaun's Adolf Hitler in Mel Brooks's* The Producers. *"Er liebt mir. Er liebt mir nicht," she recited as she pulled petals from a daisy to test his love. When she plucked out the last of the flower, she declared, "Du liebst mir nicht!" Replied Shaun: "I lieb ya, baby, I lieb ya. Now lieb me alone."*

While the critics grit their collective teeth, audience members slapped their knees. Taylor, meanwhile, made her nightly entrance as a Jewish matron in a mink coat—and rolled-down stockings.

ROSEANNE
DOMESTIC GODDESS

In the annals of In-Your-Face comedy, few will ever top the efforts of Roseanne, though it seems many will continue to try. Eschewing grace and subtlety, Roseanne parlayed her often-brilliant, always-bitchy routines into a cottage industry, even if, from time to time, her cottage seemed to be going up in flames around her.

Born in Salt Lake City in 1952, Roseanne Barr developed a facial paralysis from Bell's palsy at the age of three, then knocked her front teeth through her lip in a bicycle accident two years later. Growing up Jewish in a Mormon city—she referred to Latter-Day Saints as "the Nazi Amish"— left her picked upon and confused as an adolescent. (Roseanne also claimed to have been sexually abused as a child, allegations her family has roundly denied.) At the age of sixteen, after her involvement in a car crash that rendered her comatose for days, she suffered nightmares so severe that she was checked into the Utah State Hospital for eight months of psychiatric therapy.

Life took a long time to turn around. By the seventies she'd already had a child in the Salvation Army home for unwed mothers, before having three more children with her first husband, Bill Partland, with whom she shared a trailer in Denver. She also hooked on the side, she later told *Vanity Fair* magazine. Her first stab at comedy came when she called into a local radio talk show with a routine about housewifery and motherhood that she'd assembled herself. By 1980 she was polishing (a better term might be "toughening up") her material about domestic life, much of which was variations of Eve Arden's line in *Mildred Pierce* about alligators having the right idea about eating their young. Said Roseanne, "I

Roseanne, from a stand-up routine: "I'm a housewife. I never get out of the house. I sit at home all the time; I never do anything. I hate that word. I prefer to be called 'Domestic Goddess.' It's more descriptive." Here she is with Shelley Winters, who played her biker grandma on the Roseanne sitcom. (John Goodman played Roseanne's husband, Dan.) In 1998, Roseanne launched her own talk show and proved to be one thing that many other such daytime-TV hostesses were not—an attentive and thoughtful listener.

figure by the time my husband comes home at night, if those kids are alive I've done my job." But there was a self-deprecation to her humor, too: "I was in a dress shop," she'd say, "and I asked, 'Do you have anything that will make me look thinner?' 'Yeah. How about a week in Bangladesh?'"

What was riveting about Roseanne* was not only her jokes, which were funny, but her daring delivery, which was essentially based upon her notion of "If you don't like me, screw you." In 1983 she won a contest called the "Denver Laff-Off" and moved to Los Angeles to try her luck at the big time. She did a stint in the comedy clubs ("What do you call a really stupid woman? A man.") and Johnny Carson presented her on the *Tonight Show* in 1985, twice. Career steam was building up, and Roseanne had her own HBO pay-TV special in 1987. By the next year, ABC launched *Roseanne,* a sitcom that rewrote America's take on the family sitcom. Yes, in the early seventies the Bunker household on *All in the Family* was blunt with its dialogue, but at its heart the head of the family, Archie Bunker, was essentially a buffoon (and a male one, at that). *Roseanne* presented something different. Roseanne Conner, as her character was called, was the uneducated brain and the unsentimental heart of the household, and yet she indisputably did have a brain and a heart. (Heaven knows, if one is looking for a *Wizard of Oz*–type metaphor, she also had courage.) She played the mother of three, and then four, in the working-class suburb of Lanford, Illinois. Her sister Jackie (superbly played by Laurie Metcalf) was the Ed Norton to her Ralph Kramden. And like Roseanne herself, the show in its nine years on the air often went too far to make a point (at one juncture there was a tediously protracted story line about how Roseanne hated and resented her late father, going so far as to have her deliver an embarrassing soliloquy over his casket). But at the sitcom's core was memorable, side-splitting humor that did amplify in its own way what a loving, caring mother Roseanne was—and, perhaps, more importantly, how she was her own person. Take away the comic underpinning (as well as Roseanne's surgically enhanced and often distracting facial physical changes) and, for better or for worse, Roseanne Conner was real—and, with her commonsense approach and good humor, could have run the country.

JOANNA LUMLEY AND JENNIFER SAUNDERS POTTED PALS

Imagine Lucy and Ethel on acid. Then imagine the two of them sneaking into Little Ricky's room in the middle of the night and terrorizing the child. That, in a nutshell, was the premise of the 1992 BBC television comedy *Absolutely Fabulous,* created and written by Jennifer Saunders and her comedy partner Dawn

---

* She legally changed her name to Roseanne Arnold when she married Tom Arnold, whose career she forced on the ABC network, then legally changed again, when they divorced, to simply Roseanne.

Edina (Jennifer Saunders, left) and her daughter Saffron lived at the fictional address of 34 Claremont Avenue, in London's Holland Park. Patsy Stone (Joanna Lumley, right) was a frequent drop-in. Also visiting the overly decorated house was Edina's loony mother, June Monsoon, played by actress June Whitfield. It was seldom a pleasant visit. Edina constantly threatened her mum with the old-age home.

French, and performed—uproariously—by Saunders and Joanna Lumley, who looked less like Ethel Mertz and more like Ivana Trump. Playing the public-relations executive Edina Monsoon and the fashion editor Patsy Stone, two pals from the 1960s who never recovered from the fact that the hippie era ended (despite their love for all things with fancy labels), Saunders and Lumley ushered in a new era of bosom buddy twosomes on TV: the Unnurturing Mother and Her Drunken Sidekick. (Cybill, with Cybill Shepherd, tried to duplicate the formula, and though that show's second banana, Christine Baranski, could get a laugh reading the Salt Lake City phone book, Cybill's forced sitcom paled by comparison to the British prototype.) The one, the only *Ab Fab,* which aired on America's Comedy Central cable network,* was bravely shameless in its gags. Take the episode that ended with Eddie jumping for joy because she discovered that the rival school chum had gone blind—and therefore couldn't see how fat Eddie had become. Or Eddie dreaming she'd died and gone to heaven and met God, who turned out to be Marianne Faithful. Or when Patsy sidled up to one of the male hustlers she and Eddie hired for the night and cooed, "If I told you you had a beautiful body, would you hold it against me?" As for terrorizing "Little Ricky"—in their case, Eddie's daughter Saffron (Julia Sawalha)—it wasn't merely the matter of Patsy's constantly bullying the child for having ruined her and Eddie's reign of joie de vivre simply by Saffron's having been born, or Eddie's threat to adopt Romanian babies in order to spoil Saffron's homelife, or even Patsy's putting out cigarettes on the girl. The worst case of child abuse? Edina's sneaking into her sleeping daughter's room on the very morning Saffron was to be married, applying a depilatory tape over her upper lip, and yanking off Saffron's mustache. "It's only red for a little while, sweetie," Edina claimed as her daughter shrieked in pain. Happy Mother's Day.

ELLEN DEGENERES OVER AND OUT

On April 30, 1997, after *Time* magazine splashed her on its cover under the banner headline, "Yep, I'm Gay," Ellen DeGeneres attracted 36.2 million viewers to her ABC television sitcom, *Ellen,* to watch her come out as the first gay prime-time lead in history. It was a heady moment, all right. There was the constantly put-upon Ellen Morgan, owner of a bookstore/cafe, finally admitting to herself and to the world that she honestly found herself attracted to a woman (Laura Dern). And she honestly expressed her feelings—only to have the Dern character honestly break Ellen's heart by saying she was already involved.

Besides being a rating grabber for the show, then in its fourth season, the moment served as a litmus test of America's attitude toward homosexuality. The right-wing pulpit pounder Jerry Falwell denounced the star as "Ellen DeGenerate" (she wiped the slap away by saying that was the same stupid name she was called in school), while, according to *Entertainment Weekly* magazine, Ellen the star "was embraced by the Left, and hyped to the heavens." The *Ellen* sitcom, meanwhile, "became the network's great lavender hope."

That didn't happen. *Ellen*'s punch lines ended up taking a back seat to the social issue of Ellen being gay, and when the series was canceled exactly a year

---

* And proved to be its highest-rated show, until the animated series *South Park* came along.

after the famous episode, ABC president Robert Iger, fending off DeGeneres's constant criticism of the network for what she perceived as its lack of support, said of the fade-out of *Ellen*: "I think the audience left primarily because of sameness, not gayness."

A pity, really, because Ellen—the performer—could be funny. She was born in 1958 and had considered becoming a pro golfer before the comedy bug bit her. In the eighties she was discovered by the Showtime cable network in her native New Orleans and named by the network as the "Funniest Person in America"—which she promoted by touring the country in a Winnebago adorned with a giant schnozzola above the front bumper. While other comics' noses were bent out of shape by her having that title, Johnny Carson was so impressed by Ellen's routine that she was the first female comic ever to be invited to sit on his couch after her debut delivering her routine center stage on his *Tonight Show*.

Alas, all that seems like ancient history, or at least merely a footnote to Ellen's story, so overwhelmed as it was by the coverage of her sexuality and her personal relationship with the actress Anne Heche. Yet, ever the comedienne, when her show was preempted (and, ultimately, replaced) by ABC with a new sitcom titled *Two Guys, a Girl, and a Pizza Place*, DeGeneres couldn't resist a parting wisecrack. "Look for me in my new sitcom," she said, *"Two Girls, a Horse, and Some Wine Coolers."*

Ellen DeGeneres in 1997, fantasizing on her sitcom about declaring herself as a lesbian to a shrink played by Oprah Winfrey. Debate arose one year later as to whether coming out was a wise career move for DeGeneres. In December of 1998, Ellen announced to the Los Angeles Times that she and her partner Anne Heche were leaving Hollywood, possibly to resettle in Ojai or San Francisco.

ROSIE O'DONNELL
QUEEN OF NICE

Save for a glorious moment in 1993's *Sleepless in Seattle*—Meg Ryan mentions the dream in which she's totally naked as she walks down the street and her Patsy Kelly–like sidekick enthusiastically replies, "I love that dream"—the movie career of former stand-up comedienne Rosie O'Donnell was never going to cause Meryl Streep to lose any sleep. What a wise and splendid career move, then, when in 1996 the Long Island–reared O'Donnell debuted on daytime television with a talk show reminiscent of the Ovaltine-and-peanut-butter-and-jelly-style gabfests of Mike Douglas in the sixties. Rarely enlightening and yet ceaselessly entertaining, *The Rosie O'Donnell Show* permitted the hefty hostess to banter good-naturedly with guests who knew she'd never close in for the attack—unless they should happen to insult her imaginary love object, Tom Cruise. The approach garnered O'Donnell an impressive A-list roster of tabloid-victimized stars

Meg Ryan with Rosie O'Donnell in 1993's Sleepless in Seattle, *directed by Nora Ephron. Rosie also made her mark in the movies with Madonna in the 1992* A League of Their Own.

on the seat next to hers and the nickname, emblazoned across the front of *Newsweek,* "Queen of Nice."

Viewers happily identified with the pant-suited Rosie's appetite for junk food and her playfulness: When a self-professed household expert went on the show to demonstrate how to slice a frosted layer cake with dental floss, Rosie up and threw a piece in his face. When Scope mouthwash unkindly named O'Donnell as one of the least kissable personalities of her day, sales plummeted. Competitor Listerine stepped in to fill the void, donating money to Rosie's favorite charity every time a guest came on the show and kissed her. Those possessing puckerable lips, from Kurt Russell to Tom Cruise himself, happily complied.

A baby boomer to the core—her joy of joys was to show off to approving audiences her infinite arsenal of sixties and seventies commercial jingles lodged in her memory bank—O'Donnell was to be reckoned with as a double-barreled media force in the nineties. She not only helped return a sense of civility to the vast wasteland of daytime talk (let alone prove a bonanza to Broadway, as the popular hostess of the Great White Way's annual Tony Awards broadcasts), but she helped promote dental hygiene.

A typical Rosie O'Donnell monologue might consist of Rosie's looking into the camera and having a heart-to-heart talk with the makers of Häagen Daz ice cream, because "Mr. Manager of my supermarket" gave her the "scary news" that the company might be stopping production of its vanilla ice cream sandwich. "This is really wrong," she told Häagen Daz. "Really, really wrong."

JOAN CUSACK
THE BRIDE'S MAID

I n the best of all possible worlds, two Academy Awards would be resting on the mantelpiece of Joan Cusack—one for her Staten Island–sidekick role in 1988's *Working Girl* (wherein she and Melanie Griffith rummage through Sigourney Weaver's closet, find a dress with a pricetag on it for $6,000, and Cusack exclaims, "And it's not even leather!"), and the other for her pathetic jilted bride in 1997's *In & Out* (this time it's her husband-to-be, Kevin Kline, who's in the closet). In both cases, however, Cusack may have been a scene stealer, but the studios' advertising budgets were busily promoting other candidates for the Oscar those years. No matter: Cusack's day—and Oscar—will come.

Perhaps Cusack is able to play off-balanced comic characters so well because she comes from such a solid background. Born in New York in 1962 but raised in a bastion of Midwestern solid values—the university town of Evanston, Illinois—Cusack was the second of five children. Dad was a commercial film producer and sometime actor; younger brother John, whose films included Woody Allen's *Bullets Over Broadway,* is the leading man of the family. Joan's parents

The moment: Joan Cusack has just learned that someone from the secretarial pool (Melanie Griffith) has made it into the executive league. The film was 1988's Working Girl, *for which Cusack should have won an Oscar.*

were socially conscious, taking the children to homeless shelters to help out, and humor played an important role in the Cusack home, where Joan was reared on a diet of Monty Python and Mel Brooks movies.

It was in a children's theater that Joan "found that I could be funny," though when she went to audition for Chicago's improvisational group Second City she failed the test because, she said, "They asked me to tell a joke. And I didn't even have one." She persevered nonetheless. From 1985 to 1986 she was a regular on *Saturday Night Live,* where she developed the character of Selena, a coffee-shop owner who served Jell-O hot or cold. The situation led to larger comedy roles, including Mike Nichols's casting her for the memorable turn in *Working Girl.*

And just how does she see herself and her career taking final hold? On a sit-com of her own. "It's about me being an actress," she told an interviewer, "who moves to Chicago to have a normal life." So if not an Oscar, how about an Emmy?

JANEANE GAROFALO
HER GLIBNESS

An alumna of the stand-up school, New Jerseyite Janeane Garofalo actually premiered her act in 1969, on her first day of kindergarten. During roll call she did an entire routine criticizing the teacher for mispronouncing "Garofalo." From there hers was a natural progression to being named Class Clown in her senior high school year, and then breaking up her classmates at Providence College in Rhode Island. While testing the comedy-club waters around Boston, she kept body and soul together as a messenger, waitress, and shoe-store clerk, all the while refining her self-deprecating, urban-single shtick. "Okay," she told a reporter just as her movie career was heating up, "people don't go insane

Janeane Garofalo (here in 1996's The Truth About Cats & Dogs): "I certainly don't hate myself or have low self-esteem. I couldn't be comfortable in a femme fatale role— not that I'd be asked to play one anyway."

for me, but maybe they think I'm like someone they know, or someone they'd like to hang out and shoot the shit with." By 1990 she was shooting it on national television with Ben Stiller on his eponymous Fox network comedy show and with Garry Shandling on his superior HBO sitcom, *The Larry Sanders Show*. On the big screen she solidified her reputation as the roommate with a great personality in such small but pleasant comedies as *Reality Bites, Romy and Michele's High School Reunion,* and *The Truth About Cats & Dogs* (in which she played Uma Thurman's Cyrano to Ben Chaplin's Roxanne), and bravely took up a police pistol in the drama *Cop Land* alongside the heavy machismo barrage of Robert De Niro, Sylvester Stallone, and Harvey Keitel. Yet even as her star continued to rise, the actress-comedienne remained what she called "normal and pragmatic." In other words, her old self. "I'm not on Hollywood's A-list," admitted the half-Italian, half-Irish Garofalo (pronounced: ga-RAFF-oh-low). "That means I can pretty much speak my mind."

TART TONGUES
GENDER DEFENDERS

"Everything sets people up for competition these days. All the advertising. I don't know what they do. They sit in these rooms and they think up this stuff. It's insane. 'All right, let's think of some new names for these perfumes! O.K., you're really in competition with your best friend. You covet everything she has. You're jealous. You're bitter. You even want her husband. You're a backstabbing bitch. Envy by Gucci. Yes!'"

—Sandra Bernhard, in her 1998 one-woman Broadway show, I'm Still Here, Damn It!

With her Mick Jagger lips and "my great big Jewish ass that drives black men crazy," **Sandra Bernhard** (born 1955 in Michigan, but raised in Arizona) was never expected to be demure. After starting as a stand-up at age nineteen and supplementing her income as a Beverly Hills manicurist, she landed on her feet in 1983 playing an autograph hound in Martin Scorsese's *The*

Sandra Bernhard, on Broadway in 1998's I'm Still Here, Damn It!, *in which she said she was a new woman. She'd studied the cabala.*

King of Comedy. On TV (hot on the heels of her real-life friendship with Madonna), she joined the cast of *Roseanne* as the bisexual neighbor, until she was written out of the show. But no matter how well-delineated the role, Bernhard never seemed to get proper justice from the camera. This left her at her strongest showing live audiences just how hipper than hip she could be. Mother Teresa, John Denver, Gianni Versace, even Princess Di—you name them—were not safe from this tough cookie's barbs, even right after they'd died. Fortunately, she still has such live wires as Joni Mitchell, Gladys Knight, and The Artist Formerly Known as Prince to pick on.

*

> "I like men with pierced ears. They're better prepared for marriage. They've experienced pain and bought jewelry."
> —Rita Rudner, in her stand-up routine

Born in Miami in 1955, by the late eighties **Rita Rudner** had made a name for herself thanks to stand-up comedy shows on television and her appearances with David Letterman and the *Tonight Show.* Her style veered from the aggressive, which had been dominating female stand-up since the days of Totie Fields. Rudner's comic personality was ditsy yet feminine, poised yet easygoing. (The grace came from her days as a dancer in Broadway choruses.) "I knew so little about money," she'd joke about the hazards of being a single woman. "I used to sign my checks, 'Love, Rita.'"

*

> "Everyone thinks I'm Jewish. I'm not. Last year I got a call. 'Happy Chanukah.' I said, 'Ma, I'm not Jewish.'"
> —Joy Behar, whose Jewish surname came from her ex-husband, while her distinctly New York attitude came from the Italian neighborhoods of Brooklyn where she grew up. Daytime TV viewers were able to experience it loud and clear on the ABC program The View, which debuted in 1996 and where Behar shared the platform with other women commentators, including the very serious newswoman Barbara Walters.

> "What Asian role models were there when I grew up? There was that lady who said, 'Ancient Chinese secret, huh?' And there was that show **Kung Fu.** But they should have called it **That Guy's Not Really Chinese.**"
>
> —Margaret Cho, to Rolling Stone magazine

A Korean-American (born in 1958) who began performing stand-up at the Rose & Thistle Club above her parents' bookstore in San Francisco, **Margaret Cho** launched her career in 1991 with a stint on television's *Star Search.* In clubs her humor was a lot bluer than it was on the tube, which may have been the problem with her squeaky clean (and short-lived) 1994 ABC sitcom *All-American Girl,* in which, as a totally assimilated Asian-American, she battled the traditional hang-ups of her family. When the show was canceled it was back to the clubs for Cho, trying out new routines and even different partners.

*

> "There are so few Methodist comics, don't you know? They do a few dinner jokes and go away."
>
> —Kate Clinton, sapphic comedienne and self-styled "fumorist" who sometimes liked to joke she was President Bill Clinton's lesbian half-sister, "Hilarity" Clinton

C onsidered a cerebral Johnny Carson or a laid-back Dennis Miller, **Kate Clinton** (born in 1951) taught high school English in upstate New York for eight years before turning full-time to stand-up comedy in 1981. She did a six-month stint in 1996 writing for *The Rosie O'Donnell Show* when it was in its infancy, but declared, "Writing for television is like sausage. It tastes good, but you don't want to watch it get made." Instead, she's a sexual and political lampoonist, never pedantic, but genuinely amusing.

*

Born in 1951 (full name, Karen **Reno**) and originally billed as a radical lesbian from San Francisco, she later omitted references to homosexuality and drugs in her act. On May 11, 1998, she starred in her own HBO special, "Reno Finds Her Mom," about her search for her natural mother. "It was supposed to have aired on May 10," she said, "until HBO realized that was Mother's Day and the show had too many 'fucks' in it." And how's this for casting? In the show's dream sequences, her mother was played by Mary Tyler Moore and her fairy godmother was Lily Tomlin. Talk about great genes.

CAMERON DIAZ
SOMETHING SPECIAL

The problem with the 1997 movie *My Best Friend's Wedding* was that, try as she might, Julia Roberts could never get the audience to hate her rival, Cameron Diaz. She was just too perky, and even that wasn't a turn-off. Indeed, by the following year, when Diaz was starring in the gross-out comedy *There's Something About Mary,** absolutely everyone seemed to be in love with her, even the feminist critic Molly Haskell. "Her Mary is enchantingly, preposterously good," wrote Haskell in the *New York Observer,* "a fairy-tale princess in the middle of a castration anxiety nightmare." Haskell confessed to a weakness for

Cameron Diaz got her man in My Best Friend's Wedding *(1997). She also got the audience.*

* For which the New York Film Critics Circle named her Best Actress.

150

Mary's—and, seemingly, Cameron's—brand of "sweetness." Moreover, Haskell said of the movie, "to call it a gross-out is a misnomer, since the radiant Ms. Diaz lights it up from within, a vaccine against toxic sleaze."

Sixty years earlier, a movie like *Mary*, though no doubt less gross, would have starred Carole Lombard. (So, for that matter, would have *My Best Friend's Wedding*.) Cameron Diaz is a throwback to that kind of screwball heroine, being just as smart, spunky, and funny as the box-office names who lifted the spirits of Depression-era audiences. And like the best of the thirties movie comediennes, the young new star grew up in Southern California, in Long Beach. Her father, Emilio, worked as a foreman for Union Oil and was a second-generation Cuban-American, while her mother, an exporting agent, was of German, English, and Native American descent. Cameron had signed with the Elite modeling agency before graduating from high school, and traveled around the world on photo shoots for print ads. She made the leap to the screen when she stumbled across a copy of the script for the slyly captivating 1993 Jim Carrey comedy *The Mask* in her agent's office, and has been in movies ever since. Lucky us.

Sporting perhaps the most famous movie hair-do since Scarlett O'Hara wore a snood, Cameron Diaz starred in 1998's There's Something About Mary. *Her hair gel is actually, well, just go watch the movie.*

SELECTED BIBLIOGRAPHY

Arden, Eve. *Three Phases of Eve*. New York: St. Martin's Press, 1985.

Arnold, Roseanne. *My Lives*. New York: Ballantine Books, 1994.

Basinger, Jeanine. *A Woman's View: How Hollywood Spoke to Women, 1930–1960*. New York: Alfred A. Knopf, Inc., 1993.

Belluck, Pam. "[Joan Cusack:] A Funny Lady Who's Now a Leading Lady." *New York Times,* 14 September 1997.

Benny, Jack, and Joan Benny. *Sunday Nights at Seven: The Jack Benny Story*. New York: Warner Books, 1990.

Bram, Christopher. "Marie Dressler: The Popular Star of *Min and Bill* on Alpine Drive." *Architectural Digest,* April 1996.

Burns, George. *Living It Up*. New York: G. P. Putman, 1976.

Cagle, Jess, with reporting by Joe Flint. "As Gay As It Gets?" *Entertainment Weekly,* 8 May 1998.

Capra, Frank. *The Name Above the Title*. New York: The Macmillan Company, 1971.

Daly, Steve. "In the Money," *Entertainment Weekly,* 3 October 1997.

Degeneres, Ellen. *My Point . . . And I Do Have One*. New York: Bantam Books, 1995.

Dennen, Barry. *My Life with Barbra: A Love Story*. Amherst, N.Y.: Prometheus Books, 1997.

De Vries, Hilary. "'Darling, Listen to Me.'" *New York Times Magazine,* 26 January 1992.

Drescher, Fran. *Enter Whining*. New York: ReganBooks, 1996.

Edwards, Anne. "Hal Wallis: The Producer's Valley Farm." *Architectural Digest,* April 1992.

Franklin, Joe. *Encyclopedia of Comedians*. Secaucus, N.J.: Citadel Press, 1979.

Gill, Brendan. "Tallulah Bankhead: The Celebrated Actress in New York State." *Architectural Digest,* April 1998.

Greenfield, Jeff. *Television: The First Fifty Years*. New York: Harry N. Abrams, Inc., 1977.

Guiles, Fred Lawrence. *Marion Davies*. New York: McGraw-Hill, 1972.

Harmetz, Aljean. "Ann Sothern Dauntless." *New York Times,* 11 October 1987, Arts and Leisure.

Haskell, Molly. "Something About Beauty and Integrity." *New York Observer,* 24 August 1998.

Hepburn, Katharine. *Me*. New York: Alfred A. Knopf, Inc., 1991.

Horowitz, Susan. *Queens of Comedy*. Amsterdam: Gordon and Breach Publishers, 1997.

Kael, Pauline. *5001 Nights at the Movies*. New York: Henry Holt and Company, 1991.

Kaplan, James. "True Colors?" *New York* Magazine, 2 March 1998.

Katkov, Norman. *The Fabulous Fanny: The Story of Fanny Brice.* New York: Alfred A. Knopf, Inc., 1953.

Kendell, Elizabeth. *The Runaway Bride: Hollywood Romantic Comedy of the 1930s.* New York: Alfred A. Knopf, Inc., 1990.

Kobal, John. *People Will Talk.* New York: Alfred A. Knopf, Inc., 1985.

Krebs, Albin. "Beatrice Lillie, Comedienne and Lovable Eccentric." *New York Times,* 21 January 1989.

Lillie, Beatrice, aided and abetted by John Philip, written by James Brough. *Every Other Inch a Lady.* Garden City, N.Y.: Doubleday & Co., Inc., 1972.

Lucille Ball, First Lady of Comedy. New York: The Museum of Broadcasting, 1984.

Loy, Myrna, with James Kotsilibas-Davis. *Myrna Loy: Being and Becoming.* New York: Alfred A. Knopf, Inc., 1987.

MacIntyre, Diane. *The Silents Majority.* e-mail: www.mdle@primenet.com, 1996–97.

Marion, Frances. *Off With Their Heads.* New York: Macmillan and Company, 1972.

McNeil, Alex. *Total Television.* New York, Penguin Books USA, 1996.

Nachman, Gerald. *Raised on Radio.* New York: Pantheon Books, 1998.

Nasaw, David. "The Domestic Life: Earthly Delights." *The New Yorker,* 23 March 1998.

Novak, William, and Moshe Waldoks. *The Big Book of New American Humor: The Best of the Past Twenty-Five Years.* New York: HarperPerennial, 1990.

Parrish, James Robert. *The Slapstick Queens.* London: Thomas Yoseloff Ltd., 1973.

Radner, Gilda. *It's Always Something.* New York: Simon & Schuster, 1989.

Rudnick, Paul. *I'll Take That.* New York: Alfred A. Knopf, Inc., 1989.

Russell, Rosalind, and Chris Chase. *Life Is a Banquet.* New York: Random House, 1977.

St. John, Adela Rogers. *The Honeycomb.* Garden City, N.Y.: Doubleday & Co., 1969.

Shales, Tom. "For the Love of Lucy." *Washington Post,* 26 August 1997.

Sillman, Leonard. *Here Lies Leonard Sillman: Straightened Out At Last.* New York: The Citadel Press, 1959.

Smith, Ronald L. *Who's Who in Comedy.* New York: Facts on File, Inc., 1992.

Spehr, Paul C. *The Movies Begin: Making Movies in New Jersey 1887–1920.* Newark, N.J.: The Newark Museum, 1977.

Stand Up: Comedians on Television. New York: Harry N. Abrams, Inc., and the Museum of Television & Radio, 1996.

Stars of the Photoplay. Chicago: Photoplay Publishing Company, 1924.

Suskin, Steve. *Opening Nights on Broadway.* New York: Schirmer Books, 1990.

_____. *More Opening Nights on Broadway: A Critical Quotebook of the Musical Theatre 1965 through 1981.* New York: Schirmer Books, 1997.

Took, Barry. *Comedy Greats: A Celebration of Comic Genius Past and Present.* Wellingborough, Northamptonshire, England: Equation, 1989.

Vidor, King. *A Tree is a Tree.* New York: Samuel French, 1953.

Ward, Jack. *Television Guest Stars.* Jefferson, N.C.: McFarland & Company, Inc., 1993.

Watters, James, with photographs by Horst P. Horst. *Return Engagement: Faces to Remember—Then & Now.* New York: Clarkson N. Potter, 1984.

West, Mae. *Goodness Had Nothing to Do with It.* New York: Belvedere Publishers, 1981.

_____. *Three Plays by Mae West.* Ed. Lillian Schlissel. New York: Routledge, 1997.

Wilk, Max. *Golden Age of Television: Notes from Survivors.* Mount Kisco, N.Y.: Moyer Bell Limited, 1989.

Worth, Larry. "[Janeane Garofalo:] Not Just Another Funny Face." *New York Post,* 27 September 1997.

Ziegfeld, Richard, and Paulette Ziegfeld. *The Ziegfeld Touch: The Life and Times of Florenz Ziegfeld, Jr.* New York: Harry N. Abrams, Inc., 1993.

Zimmerman, Paul D., and Burt Goldblatt. *The Marx Brothers at the Movies.* New York: G. P. Putnam's Sons, 1968.

ACKNOWLEDGMENTS

At Harry N. Abrams, Inc.: Paul Gottlieb, for his years of patience on this book and a previous one, as well as those two or three that didn't quite make it to fruition (also for carving the turkey at the author's last book party); Carol Morgan, for her valuable suggestions at any and all hours; Ruth Peltason, for her sterling idea and her stainless editing; and the designer Molly Shields, for her "good looks."

In New York: Vernel Bagneris, for sharing his knowledge of the Theater Owners Booking Association; Sandra Birnhak, president of Worldview Entertainment, Inc., which owns the Killian Collection of silent movies, for the quick fix of Sennett heroines; Mary Corliss, of the Stills Department of the Museum of Modern Art, for her good taste, her constant friendship, and the welcome supply of champagne; Bob Cosenza, of the Kobal Collection, for his impeccable taste; Judith Crist, for possessing the most impressive private library of film books on either coast and eschewing a blue pencil in favor of a red pen; Jean Doumanian, for providing an insight or two; Brandon Judell, for sharing his consummate knowledge of the life and times of ZaSu Pitts; Margaret Denk and Nina Pinksy, for keeping the author from conking out in the last stretch; Martha Kaplan, for behaving sensibly at all times (a characteristic her client does not share); the Brothers Mandlebaum, Ron and Howard, of Photofest, for their deft picture research; the late Marcella Rabwin, for expounding upon Lucille Ball, Tallulah Bankhead, and Carole Lombard; Anna Sosenko, for sharing her memories of Fanny Brice and show business in general; John Springer, for his encyclopedic mind; and Heather White, for turning me onto previously undiscovered photographic archives.

In Bedford, New York: The film preservationist Robert A. Harris, my "brother" (our "father" was David Lean), for letting this madman ransack his archives.

In Los Angeles: Joan Cohen, for picking up the photos at the Academy; and Peggy Glance, for the use of the silver T-Bird.

In Sitges, Spain: Sir John Mills, for sharing his memories of Beatrice Lillie.

At the New York Public Library for the Performing Arts in Lincoln Center: Christine Karatnytsky, in the Billy Rose Theater Collection, for her kind and gracious assistance.

At the Margaret Herrick Library, Center for Motion Picture Study, in Beverly Hills: Stacey Behlmer, for facilitating the photo research and for her boundless enthusiasm and movie scholarship.

INDEX